A History of the Metropolitan Railway

The Circle and the lines extended north to Rickmansworth

Lamplight Publications

260 Colwell Drive, Witney, Oxon OX28 5LW

First published 2003

ISBN 1 899246 07 X

Designed and typeset by Lamplight Publications.
Printed and bound by the Alden Press at Oxford

A History of the
METROPOLITAN RAILWAY

The Circle and the extended lines to Rickmansworth

by Bill Simpson

Lamplight Publications

Original crest of the Metropolitan Railway that appeared on early electric stock.

METROPOLITAN RAILWAY
Extension Lines

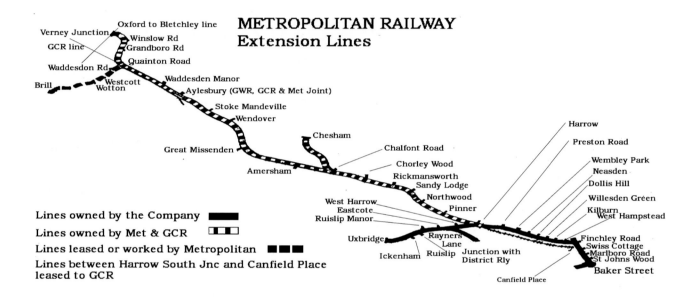

Oxford to Bletchley line
Verney Junction
Winslow Rd
GCR line
Grandboro Rd
Waddesdon Rd
Quainton Road
Waddesden Manor
Brill
Westcott
Wotton
Aylesbury (GWR, GCR & Met Joint)
Stoke Mandeville
Wendover
Chesham
Great Missenden
Chalfont Road
Chorley Wood
Rickmansworth
Amersham
Sandy Lodge
West Harrow
Northwood
Eastcote
Pinner
Ruislip Manor
Harrow
Preston Road
Wembley Park
Neasden
Dollis Hill
Willesden Green
Kilburn
West Hampstead
Uxbridge
Rayners Lane
Ickenham
Ruislip
Junction with District Rly
Finchley Road
Swiss Cottage
Marlboro Road
St Johns Wood
Baker Street
Canfield Place

Lines owned by the Company
Lines owned by Met & GCR
Lines leased or worked by Metropolitan
Lines between Harrow South Jnc and Canfield Place leased to GCR

METROPOLITAN RAILWAY
Circle Lines

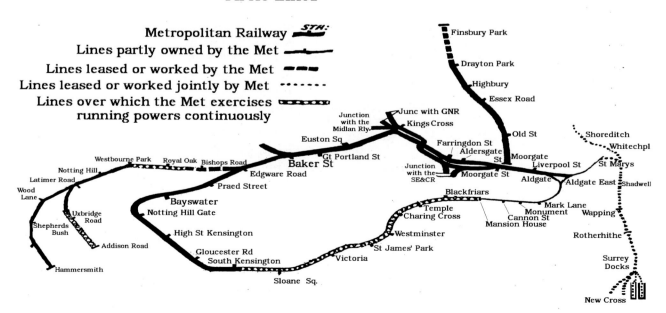

Metropolitan Railway
Lines partly owned by the Met
Lines leased or worked by the Met
Lines leased or worked jointly by Met
Lines over which the Met exercises running powers continuously

Finsbury Park
Drayton Park
Highbury
Essex Road
Junction with the Midlan Rly.
Junc with GNR
Kings Cross
Euston Sq
Westbourne Park
Royal Oak
Bishops Road
Gt Portland St
Baker St
Notting Hill
Edgware Road
Latimer Road
Praed Street
Wood Lane
Bayswater
Uxbridge Road
Notting Hill Gate
Shepherds Bush
Addison Road
High St Kensington
Gloucester Rd
South Kensington
Hammersmith
Sloane Sq.
Old St
Farringdon St
Aldersgate St
Junction with the SE&CR
Moorgate St
Moorgate
Liverpool St
Aldgate
Blackfriars
Temple
Charing Cross
Mark Lane
Cannon St
Mansion House
Monument
Westminster
St James' Park
Victoria
Shoreditch
Whitechpl
St Marys
Aldgate East
Shadwell
Wapping
Rotherhithe
Surrey Docks
New Cross

Foreword

The history of the Metropolitan Railway is rich in detail, it could hardly be anything but with such an immense subject as the City of London as its basis. It is difficult now to imagine the city without its underground, serving both in war and peace time as a dependable public service.

The late poet laureate Sir John Betjeman was a city man that loved the country and held the view that, 'we live by contrast'. The Metropolitan Railway brought about probably the greatest railway contrast in the British Isles. Its London lines connected the glamour of the west end with the hard workaday world of the city and the docks and in doing so became a continuous pastiche of the life and history of the city for nearly one hundred and fifty years.

At first it ran with steam locomotives that burst vividly into sunlight in the openings between the sub-surface sections. These were eventually replaced with electric trains that went flashing into the darkness. Lines probed out to Hammersmith and to New Cross, whilst the system continued to spread through various other connections.

Energies of its leaders drove it north, leaving the city through the developing suburbs that thinned away to reach the rural wooded Chilterns. Eventually, arriving in remotest Buckinghamshire at Verney Junction. Or even more rustically, at the foot of the hill top village of Brill, after having changed into a tiny train at Quainton Road, contrast indeed!

This first of three volumes begins the study as far as Rickmansworth. The second, from there to Aylesbury, with a final volume on the lines north of that town.

Most of the Metropolitan Railway lines remain as part of London Transport as far as Amersham. Beyond we can still ride to Aylesbury on services provided by Chiltern Railways, who are largely responsible for the superb restoration and vitality of the appearance of stations on the northern section.

What began with the Metropolitan is now a complex organisation of lines and stations, a virtual city underground, confirming the vision of Charles Pearson beyond what he could ever have imagined. The object of his endeavour won against the odds.

Bill Simpson
Bicester 2003

Acknowledgments

I would like to make special mention of the friendship and support of Mike Crosbie, not only on this book but also on my former work *The Brill Tramway*. His wealth of knowledge of London's railways provided the support and confident help so essential in the isolation of authorship.

I would also like to acknowledge the dedicated work of the late Ken Benest who did so much to collate and contribute valuable material on London's railways.

The following have generously contributed time and material without which I could not have produced the first volume and I am very grateful for this.

Eric Fenton, Secretary, (London Underground Society), Austin Harland, David Hibbert (London Underground Society), Simon Murphy (London's Transport Museum), John Reed, Dudley Rudd, Ron White (Colourviews), The staff of Uxbridge and Watford public libraries. The numerous owners of illustrations that have supported my efforts and shown every consideration. They are credited appropriately throughout the book.

In the distance, shaded by haze, Wren's masterpiece of St Paul's Cathedral that so successfully resolves the visual emphasis of the City of London, after the great fire. It now looks down on another insurrection, that of railways as they are determinedly forced across the city. Not least the excavations of the Metropolitan with the first underground lines seen here.

London's Transport Museum

Contents

Baker Street not too dissimilar from the present day appearance, it was restored from its strip lighting and festoons of posterboards in 1983. The openings originally emitted daylight, quite impossible now with Chiltern Court above. The present imitation gasoliers are, however, very effective. Here it is seen with one feature irrelevant to restoration, the Great Western Railway broad gauge tracks.

London's Museums Collection

Chapter One

The CIRCLE

At the time of the Coronation of Queen Victoria in 1838 London was a very compact city, it clutched on to the commerce of the River Thames as it had done for thousands of years. River Navigations brought produce from the country and this was aided by the permeating influence of canals in the seventeenth century. The Regents Canal was built as an extension from the Grand Junction Canal at Paddington to the Docks. It was proposed at one point to turn this waterway into a railway. Thankfully not and today it forms a tranquil respite from the domination of both roads and railways.

Such rapid growth was of course as a consequence of the development of the railways, with road transport playing a supplementary role, with horse drawn carts, trams and omnibuses. Throughout her reign she witnessed the greatest urban development ever seen, producing a city well worthy of the hub of a mighty empire.

Naturally many of the great trunk line railway companies, reaching to the furthest corners of the land at this period, accessed the capital and built their own goods and passenger termini in a ring around it, eventually consolidating as; London Bridge (1836), Euston LNWR (1837), Paddington GWR (1838), Fenchurch Street LTSR (1841), Waterloo (Nine Elms) LSWR (1848), Kings Cross GNR (1852), Victoria LBSCR (1860/2), Charing Cross (1864), SER Cannon Street (1866), St Pancras Midland Railway (1868), Liverpool Street GER (1874), Marylebone GCR (1899). It was decreed by a Royal Commission that no railway shall proceed closer into the capital than the boundaries of Marylebone Road, City Road, Finsbury Square and Bishopsgate Street. That was until the London Chatham & Dover Railway brazenly went directly across the city from Blackfriars to Ludgate Hill to join the Met at Farringdon Street on January 1, 1866.

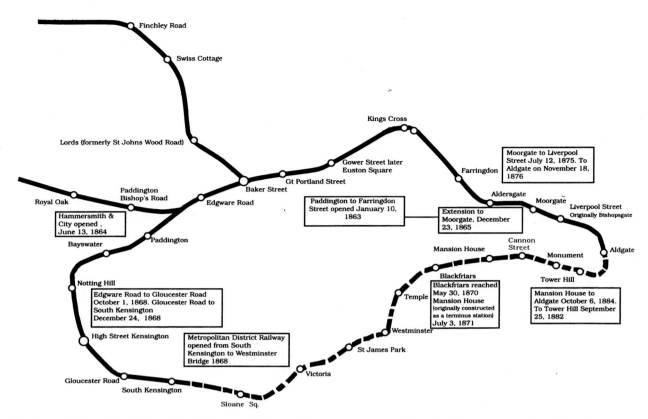

The Inner Circle of the Metropolitan Railway which was often run as a terminal loop by the two companies with trains running off from it. A Middle Circle ran, Moorgate, Paddington, Addison Road, Earls Court. With an Outer Circle, Broad Street, Camden Town, Willesden Junction and Addison Road

Eventually joined by the South Eastern & Chatham Railway. Later, in 1900, the Central London Railway would cross from east to west.

In consequence the railways were bringing passengers into this restricted area. To enable some pace of movement there came the development of omnibuses.

In 1829 George Shillibeer's omnibuses were carrying twenty passengers in each vehicle between rail termini. There followed an increasing number running between Paddington Green and the Bank of England. In the following ten years there were another 600 services introduced. By 1865 200,000 people were entering the city daily on foot with 7000 daily bus journeys being made.

Much was made of the London of the mid 19th century with railways bringing so much commerce and movement into this circle of termini. Carts, omnibuses, coaches and all the horse drawn transport, all moving in opposing directions. The noises of hoofs, steel wheels on cobbles and the shouts of drivers must have been appalling, not to mention the droppings from thousands of horses. It was complained of that it took more time to cross the city than it did to reach Oxford on the train.

The inspired thinking of Sir Joseph Paxton, designer of the Crystal Palace, produced a scheme for a railway riding under an arcaded thoroughfare, forming a connecting circle. This was pictorially described as 'The Crystal Way'. Consideration was given to an atmospheric system, or winding engines, but none of these options were taken up, and the 'Crystal Way' remained an unrealised image of contrasting elegance. Apart from the congestion of the streets, these termini needed a common link, in order to prove a successful transport system for the city.

In 1837 a George Remington managed to get an Act for a railway from Camden Town to the church of St Sepulchre at Holborn, over an immense viaduct. This proposal received little support. The prospect then re-emerged as a cutting and received little more support, disparagingly called 'The Ditch'. Public reaction was very hostile and the plan was dropped.

The first serious scheme to go underground was the Metropolitan City Terminus Company with a capital of £600,000 in 60,000 shares of £10 each on the deposit of £1 a share. This company foundered because it could not strike common accord with the City Improvements Committee.

In 1853 came the North Metropolitan Railway; (Bayswater, Paddington & Holborn Bridge Railway). It took over the interests of the

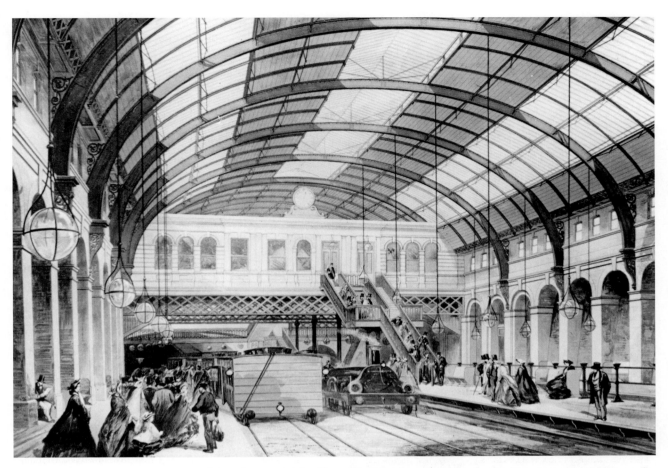

The original station at Kings Cross with broad gauge tracks. The splendid arch canopy of iron and glass shows clearly the work marvelled at by the VIP's on the special train before the opening. With alterations to the tramway on the road above and the work on Widened Lines the station had to be rebuilt to the more prosaic assembly of flat canopies.

London's Museums Collection

former enterprise for 4¼ mile line. The capital for this company was established at £1,000,000 into 100,000 shares of £10 with £600,000 held by various parties and sizeable £175,000 held by the Great Western Railway who wished to gain some influence over the scheme. The 1853 Bill was unopposed but an extension Bill of 1854 was tenaciously opposed by the City Corporation, GWR, LNWR, GNR, St Bartholomews Hospital, the Reverend Byrne, Justices of Middlesex, William Cubitt, Commissioners for Sewers, etc. The gist of the opposition was that the amount apportioned for compensation was too small at £353,000, opportunists abounded. A derelict property suddenly claimed the distinction of a palace, if the railway was planning to tunnel beneath it. The proposers tried earnestly to route their line under roads to avoid this.

However the Metropolitan were well served by their engineer John Fowler and architect J Hargreaves-Stevens, both were experienced articulate men and could hold their corner in debate.

The proposed line was to be from Farringdon Street to join with the GWR at a place called Bishop's Road close by their Paddington terminus. The GWR were enthusiastic, they had good reason to be, Paddington was the furthest west, set a little more remotely from the clutch of stations around Euston and beyond. A link putting them on a par with all others was an obvious advantage. It would also validate their own famous broad gauge of 7ft ¼ in, although, out in the country this gauge choice was now beginning to falter. Problems at Oxford and Banbury brought about mixed gauge compromises.

The solicitor to the Corporation of the City of London, a Charles Pearson was a strong advocate for railways. He was very keen on the railway link idea and advocated that it would be best, but expensive, to build the railway beneath the streets. He was behind the Bayswater, Paddington & Holborn Bridge Railway. This railway would run from Paddington to the Post Office at St Martin's le Grand just over three miles long, and would be the first underground railway in the world. An advantage of Pearson's plan was that it included improvements to Holborn Hill and raised the level of the Fleet Valley by 17ft 6ins

Charles Pearson, untiring champion of an ideal, the world's first underground railway.

London's Museums Collection

to the level of St Sepulchre's Church and St Andrews on the other. Pearson's dedication proved convincing by his spending £8,000 of his own money pursuing the scheme, no trifling sum in 1859.

A meeting was called at the offices of a solicitor, one William Burchill for January 10, 1853.

At this meeting the name 'North Metropolitan Railway' was adopted and submitted for the incorporated Act of parliament which received the Royal Assent on August 15, 1853. The plans sanctioned were for a railway to be built under New Road (Euston Road) on a direct line between Paddington and Kings Cross, the GWR were of course at Paddington and the Great Northern had recently extended its line from Maiden Vale (1850) to their terminus at Kings Cross. Between them both was the mighty edifice of the London & Birmingham Railway at Euston Square. The alignment of the new railway was about to run beneath the new road across north

London which was a natural progression between them. The first Act was for Paddington to Kings Cross, the Act for the section from Kings Cross to Holborn Bridge (Farringdon Street) was submitted as a separate undertaking and was not at the same time successful in parliament. Nevertheless the railway existed as an entity on which progress would now be sought. An essential feature on the eastern line was the clearance of land for the development of the new Smithfield market near Farringdon Street. This brought about the intensively used underground rail yard beneath the market

The GWR had been keen from the outset and had agreed to subscribe £175,000 on securement of the Act. An obvious stipulation being that the gauge for the line, chosen at 4ft 8½ ins should also be aligned with the GWR's 7ft ¼in broad gauge, a mixed gauge system.

The gauge question had been hotly contested by the railways in the 1850's. The first trunk route the London & Birmingham Railway was built by Robert Stephenson in his father's adopted gauge of 4ft 8½in. Isambard Kingdom Brunel, Engineer of the GWR favoured the broad gauge on his system. The retention of mixed gauge was a necessary evil for the GWR.

Obviously the young North Metropolitan Railway would acquiesce with such a substantial a supporting company. With the weight of this support the NMR were more successful on a second attempt to secure the outstanding section of the line from Kings Cross to Farringdon Street. An Act for this received the Royal Assent on August 7, 1854. The company also reincorporated itself now as the Metropolitan Railway Company. The one significant amendment was that the original line would require to go under Cold Bath Fields Prison, therefore leave was obtained to divert the line from its original course to go to the Post Office to end at Farringdon Street instead.

Not to miss an opportunity the GNR sought powers to subscribe the sum of £175,000 in return for running powers to the city. This money was never actually subscribed but in 1860 the Met were persuaded to take a smaller sum to form a junction with the GNR at Kings Cross. Fortuitous in view of the subsequent action taken by the GWR after opening.

Although the railway was projected no great distance as railways go, just over three miles, going beneath street level, the required capital of one million pounds was slow to accumulate. Fear of existing railways was prevalent, with good reason. Engines move along at great speed carrying their own furnace from which they expire sparks onto the huddled passengers in little more than open boxes, made of wood. It

692   THE ILLUSTRATED LONDON NEWS   [Dec. 27, 1862

From the Illustrated London News at the time of opening, the architectural mark made by the new railway on the streets of London. The stations became less dominating with building in-fill. But many others would follow, so much so that a London without its Underground is now unimaginable. Note illustration on left of cross-over junction that was objected to by the inspecting officer of the Board of Trade Colonel Yolland, who remarked that the junction was too close to the walls.

London's Museums Collection

Steam at Notting Hill Gate on April 25, 1954, engine no L52 former 'F' class no 93 passes through with an engineers train. The locomotive was withdrawn in 1962 and subsequently scrapped in 1964.

John Edgington

does not require a great stretch of the imagination to envisage what would be in the public's mind in the confines of a continuous tunnel where death by suffocation or fire would be very possible.

Nevertheless Charles Pearson held to his obsession and from 1850 to 1860 railway technology made considerable advances with 'lock and block' signalling system. Also locomotives being built at this time were far more able to perform starts with the acceleration required on a compact railway.

The Metropolitan Railway issued a Prospectus on July 15, 1856 keeping the plan uppermost in people's minds. Charles Pearson appealed directly to the populace with the prospect of cheap tickets. It must have seemed somewhat tempting to think of being able to move around cheaply and easily as the outer development of the city began to sprawl towards suburbs, especially for employment.

What enforced confidence was when the City of London Corporation decided to take a hand in investment to the tune of £200,000. This was a turning point and gradually the required capital was reached.

An associate of the Met's solicitor Burchill took out a large shareholding in the Met, this was one John Parson. He had been solicitor of the Oxford, Worcester & Wolverhampton Railway which at the outset had been a sibling of the GWR, to be built in the broad gauge.

Parson quarrelled with the GWR and used the power and influence of a large rival, the London & North Western Railway, accessing Euston in standard gauge from their line, instead of Paddington. It would bring no joy at Paddington to know that Parson had entered the scene. Further, in February 1860 he became deputy chairman and by May 1865 he was chairman.

By an Act of August 8, 1859 Farringdon Street had been adopted as the eastern terminus, not the Post Office. The Chief Engineer was to be John Fowler (later Sir John Fowler) with resident Engineer T Marr Johnson. Contractor for the line was Smith & Knight for the section from Bishop's Road, Paddington to Euston Square. From there to Victoria Street was under the control of one John Jay.

Rails were of iron with steel surfaces to the depth of one sixteenth of an inch, steel was still an expensive alloy, from the Dodd process. They were of the Vignoles pattern and weighed 62lbs a yard and were bolted in GWR style to longitudinal sleepers. This process worked well enough on straight rail but predictably the binding on curves soon wore it away. Stress at these points would then cause rail damage like splitting and cracking. Fortunately technology was not too far behind and the Bessemer conversion process in 1866 brought cheap steel in plentiful supply and the line was relaid with all steel rails with a flange of $6^{3}/_{8}$, much more

Paddington (Praed Street) as it looked at its opening in October 1868.

Railway Gazette

sufficient unto the task of a short intensively used line. At the same time the more stable cross-sleepers were laid. Eventually all of the line was relaid with steel bullhead rail of 86lb per yard. There was also heavier rail used of 95 and 100 lb per yard in manganese steel in the heaviest used areas like Baker Street.

Farringdon Street is outside the boundary of the City of London and was at first called Victoria Street. The new name was adopted from May 22, 1863.

Construction contracts for the railway were placed in December 1859. Naturally construction began at Paddington so that the spoil could be removed by rail. This transpired to be the ground of Chelsea Football Club at Lillie Bridge, before they moved to Stamford Bridge in 1905. The contracts required the railway to be completed in 21 months. Between Paddington and Kings Cross, the system adopted was to 'cut and cover' which was of course a great deal easier than tunnelling. The roof was staunchly supported by huge ribs of wrought iron. London was in turmoil as the roads were trenched and pierced with hundreds of timbers shuttering on a long perspective of men digging and lifting soil and clay like a colony of ants. Beyond Kings Cross it was possible for much of the line to be in open cutting, but it did include the 600 yard long Coppice Row tunnel near Farringdon Street.

The Fleet Prison was demolished to increase space for the workings. Inevitably some sections did collapse but repairs were speedily put in hand. Rather spectacularly, the Fleet Ditch sewer burst into the works on June 18, 1862 and

filled a section to 10ft deep near Farringdon Street. Men were lowered in baskets to break holes in the brickwork abutments to drain the waters into excavations on each side. As they were about this operation some arching gave way for several hundred yards. This forced piling from its restraint and all manner of detritus of excavation slid into this ditch including locomotives and trucks. A gas main ruptured nearby and a mausoleum collapsed from St Peters burial ground and human remains entered the suppurating morass. The prospect of this restored to the human environment in the form of a canal in the summer month of June is probably something that one does not want to imagine. Whatever, the men of the Metropolitan were not to be daunted, John Jay the contractor and his men banished the Fleet Ditch to its own course once more.

A trial train ran on August 30, 1862 after a preliminary Board of Trade inspection. This must have been prior to some works of improvement as the official inspection by Colonel Yolland did not take place until December 22. He required certain signalling alterations to be installed. Although the Met was to have the usual mechanical type it was the first railway to be worked on the absolute 'block' system throughout from the beginning and totally interlocked. The opening of the line provided the first occasion for block telegraph instruments to be used designed by C E Spagnoletti, the Telegraph Superintendent of the GWR. This was to become standard on the GWR as the Disc Block Telegraph Instrument. His device was a three wire three position disc

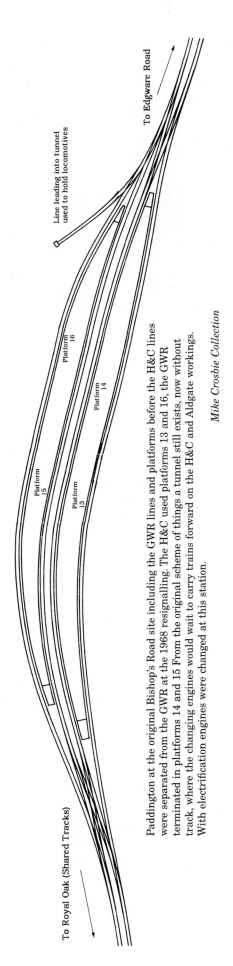

To Edgware Road

Line leading into tunnel
used to hold locomotives

Platform 16

Platform 14

Platform 15

Platform 13

Mike Crosbie Collection

Paddington at the original Bishop's Road site including the GWR lines and platforms before the H&C lines were separated from the GWR at the 1968 resignalling. The H&C used platforms 13 and 16, the GWR terminated in platforms 14 and 15 From the original scheme of things a tunnel still exists, now without track, where the changing engines would wait to carry trains forward on the H&C and Aldgate workings. With electrification engines were changed at this station.

To Royal Oak (Shared Tracks)

indicator with two differently toned bells referring to 'up' and 'down' line respectively. This was an improvement to the earlier indicator by Mr Edwin Clarke of the LNWR. The dial had a green blind with an oblong aperture through which the disc showed full on, indicating 'line clear'; with the red disc showing full on indicating 'Train on Line'. Below this were two keys for actuating the above signals, one red and one white. The corresponding words to these appeared in the opening on the face of the dial.

The length of the 'block' sections was at first governed by the distance between stations. But as the density of traffic increased the longer sections had to be subdivided and loco condensing places carefully mapped out to prevent the tunnel signals being completely obscured.

Electric automatic signalling by means of track circuits, was brought into use between Praed Street and Notting Hill Gate in January 1908. By the Autumn of 1909 the Circle Line from South Kensington to Aldgate was equipped with the new method of signalling. The same system with upper quadrant semaphores was installed between Baker Street and Neasden on the northern extension in November 1910. Power signal frames with track circuit illuminated diagrams were opened at Praed Street Junction on July 26, 1908. Further at Aldgate on September 26, 1909 and at Baker Street on January 4, 1913. Train description apparatus was installed on the 'down' line between Baker Street and Willesden Green.

Telegraphic communication on the Met was taken over by the Post Office on January 28, 1870. As the new lines were being built Wheatstone proposed to install private speaking instruments between their West End residences and City Offices. For this, in anticipation of the new telephone service, a subscription of 5 pounds 5 shillings a year was suggested.

On December 30, Colonel Yolland gave general approval, subject to outstanding works being attended to. His final inspection came on January 3, 1863.

At last a term of trial was over and a train was run carrying the Directors accompanied by a party of 600 on Friday January 9, 1863 from Bishop's Road to Farringdon Street, in two trains leaving soon after 1 pm. They took two hours and ten minutes but it must be added that stops were made at Edgware Road, Baker Street, Portland Road (this became Great Portland Street on March 1, 1917). Also at this point was a ventilation shaft. At Kings Cross, the party stopped to admire and enthuse over

Edgware Road station in the 1960's. The first locomotive stabling point and works on the Metropolitan was once at this station.

London Underground Railway Society

the impressive work of the engineers and their men. The gas lit stations were admired for the way that looked, not so much underground, but like a well lit street at night.

At Farringdon Street a specially built temporary hall of 250ft long and 50ft wide enclosed the assemblage 350 guests along with their banquet, which was garnished with the usual fine speeches. Nevertheless, it was the first railway of its type in the world and was no little credit to the determination and fortitude of the men that had seen it through. All were impressed and understood the importance of what had been achieved. Mr Gladstone, Duke of Sutherland, Earl Grosvenor and Mr Robert Lowe, Chancellor of the Exchequer all

Notting Hill Gate station in the broad gauge shortly before opening, note signalling contractor Saxby & Farmer signal on left a slotted post semaphore.

London Undergrpound Railway Society

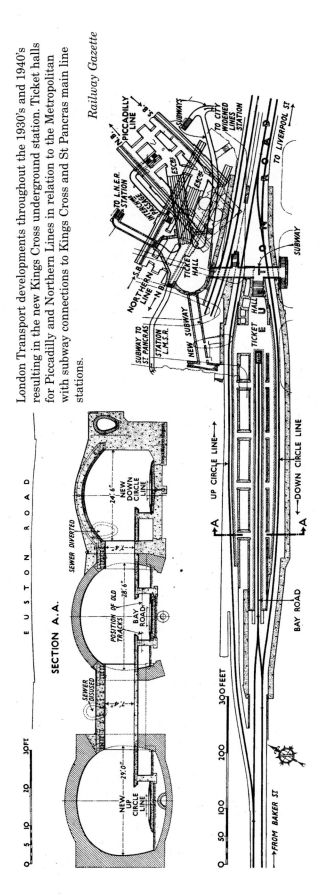

London Transport developments throughout the 1930's and 1940's resulting in the new Kings Cross underground station. Ticket halls for Piccadilly and Northern Lines in relation to the Metropolitan with subway connections to Kings Cross and St Pancras main line stations.

Railway Gazette

travelling in the most basic open wagons with Charles Pearson and John Fowler introducing them to the line. These men had no doubt of what they were witnessing, but it would have been a test of their imaginations to conceive of what London has achieved today in terms of an underground railway system.

Public traffic began on January 10, 1863 and the men of the Metropolitan must have been amazed themselves to carry 38,000 people along the line in one day, so much for the fear of the subterranean railway. Engines and rolling stock were supplied by the GWR on the broad gauge. So great was the demand to use the railway that the GWR employed trains of narrow gauge engines and carriages. Kings Cross was the most popular station on the line where the new GNR station was beheld in all its impressive grandeur. A journey time took between thirty-three and forty minutes and crowds pushed and swayed about in a hysteria of enthusiasm to use the railway. On completion of the first week it had carried 224,000 people; Saturday 38,000, Sunday 33,000, Monday 26,000, Tuesday 21,000, Wednesday 25,000, Thursday 26,000, Friday 25,000 and Saturday 30,000. The Met took £2,400 per week over the first three weeks. Single fares were 6d, (2½p), first class with 4d(2p) second class and 3d(1¼p) third with returns 9d(4¼p), 6d(2½p) and 5d(2¼p) respectively. Annual season tickets were available £8 first and £5/10 shillings second. From May 1864 the Metropolitan also made available cheap early morning workmen's fares of 3d return. This was an intelligent and shrewd move as it was obvious to the Metropolitan that there was a huge potential in the capital for the working masses to move their employment without restriction. The second class was abolished on September 24, 1905.

On October 1, 1863 the GWR began a service between Farringdon Street and Windsor but suspended this at the end of the year. In the same month GNR rails were connected to the Met.

After the first week the staff were completely exhausted by working extra hours. The railway had organised itself to run a train every ten minutes, no light undertaking equalled by few railways at the time. One problem was with the engines, the engine crews did their best to rule out exhausting from the engine along the underground sections, if even for their own sakes. But heavy condensing had to be done between Kings Cross and Edgware Road and at pace, so much so that the water in the tanks was at boiling point. This was dangerous as the tanks had no safety valves and once in the open air steam was expired as much as possible to reduce the heat on the engine. Nevertheless, an

Baker Street station in 1908, Chiltern Court was not built until two years later. Neverthless the signs and notices confidently claim patronage. Note the 'Underground' railway services advertised.

London's Transport Museum

Baker Street at platform level with a MetroVic loco no 7 'Edmund Burke' reversing into the siding for Chiltern Court. No 16 'Oliver Goldsmith' of the same class waits in the distance.

London's Transport Museum

Chiltern Court the splendid edifice above Baker Street completed in 1913, this view in 1933. It had a restaurant to dine 250 people with its 1000 rooms. An example that followed with other stations in subsequent years of placing a building above, with the underground this is a great deal easier than with stations above ground. The entrance on the corner remains from the original station

London's Transport Museum

attempt was made to run the trains faster to cover the entire line in 18 minutes.

Gooch had designed the tank engines for working the Met, these were 2-4-0 outside cylinders (16in x 24in). twenty-two were built, the first six by Vulcan Foundry at Newton-le-Willows. These were named after flying insects, Bee, Mosquito, Gnat, Hornet, Locust and Wasp. A further six were built by Kitson of Leeds and were called Czar, Kaiser, Khan, Shah, Mogul and Bey. Was there any Peninne rivalry between the two groups, one wonders? That as it may, the remaining ten were built in Wiltshire at the GWR works at Swindon. The engines must have been impressive locos of their time, with 6ft diameter coupled wheels and 3ft 6in diameter leading wheels. They had no cabs only weatherboards. However judging by the situation in traffic their water tanks would need to be increased in size to try and stop overheating.

A proposed locomotive type that failed was the concept of John Fowler, who designed a loco without a fire, a hot-brick loco, built by Robert Stephenson & Co in 1861. He maintained that a sufficient volume of hot steam could be infused by the bricks and the engine would then

be able to continue without exhausting for a single journey. It was tried on the GWR main line on October 10, 1861 where it was a failure. More successfully it was tried again between Paddington (Bishop's Road) and the Edgware Road on November 28 1861. But the concept was too novel and would require more development and the Metropolitan did not have time to ponder on some esoteric prototype, they needed a fleet at once. So conventional locos were allotted the task of running the railway. In truth 'Fowler's Ghost', as it was called, was probably a concept presented more for public reassurance and support to get the Act passed rather than a serious undertaking, engineers must have had their doubts. The problem of fumes was never quite as bad as it was feared with judicious enginemanship and the supplanting of coal for coke after six years. The coke used was from Durham coal, burnt in coke ovens to remove sulphur. It was superseded by South Wales semi-anthracite coal. One signalman enclosed in the gloomy confines of Euston underground lived and worked there for twenty-seven years and retired in good health. The matter was of course no problem at all when, eventually electrification arrived.

Kings Cross station undergoing permanent way work in the mid 1970's The pointwork at Kings Cross between the station and the tunnels was so complicated that trains had to move very slowly, this modification is to simplify it. York Road station platform can be seen on the extreme left with diesel locomotive at the entrance to the tunnel. Over on the extreme right with St Pancras in the background is the Hotel curve station, both of course no longer exist. The 'Thameslink' services use the Widened Lines tunnels under St Pancras station. The space alongside the class 47 in the centre was occupied by a 232 lever frame signalbox, this was removed on replacement with the power box in 1973.

Early Coaches of the Metropolitan

Early coaches, supplied by Brown, Marshalls of Birmingham, were of the GWR type, known as 'Long Charleys' and comprised of 35 eight-wheeled compartment carriages of 42ft over buffers. The two pairs of wheels were grouped at each end on a rigid wheelbase. This was the radial system that allowed fixed wheel base for the inside pairs whilst the outside pairs could follow the track curve, The wheels were 6ft from the coach ends. First class carriages were divided into six compartments giving a total seating capacity of 48. Second and third class were divided into eight compartments allowing seating for eighty. Each coach when fully loaded weighed 17 tons. Six of the coaches were old stock but new ones were, six first class, with nine composite which included first and second; also fourteen third class vehicles. This shows that the Met knew precisely where their future lay, cheap mass movement which meant many working people of modest means. It was the first company in London to introduce cheap fares for working people in May 1864 without statutory requirement. They could buy tickets at three pence, for the morning 5.30 and 5.40 from Bishops Road which were filled to capacity. They were able to return by any train, thus the first commuters had started and the working habits of the nation were in process of unremitting change.

New coaches had been built by The Ashbury

Railway Carriage & Iron and the Oldbury Carriage Co (1863) and were 10ft 6in wide. The second and third class compartments carried six each side. One uneasy factor which one would not want to dwell upon, is that these timber vehicles were coal gas lit, the gas being contained in tanks of collapsible bellows on the roof of each carriage. These wooden boxes were weighted on the top and as the weight descended an indicator on the side informed staff if it was full 'F' or empty 'E', or perhaps somewhere between. Bags were refilled from holders situated at each end of the line. the Julius Pintsch system allowed coal gas to be stored under pressure, originally oil lamps had been used. Spectacularly coaches first used on the Met had carpets and upholstered seats for all classes. This amazed their passengers having to suffer the rudimentary stock of the larger trunk railways. It was of course part of the psychology of reassurance and it worked! Smoking compartments were catered for, as if there was not enough smoke on the underground.

New Oldbury four-wheel coaches came to the Met in 1870, close coupled in pairs making nearly 44ft. First class compartments had four passengers on each side with arm rests.

At first the coaches were fitted with Newall's handbrake operated from the guard's compartment on wooden brake blocks on four wheels. The distinct smell of the underground at the time was in fact attributed as much to the smell of burning brakes as locomotives. From

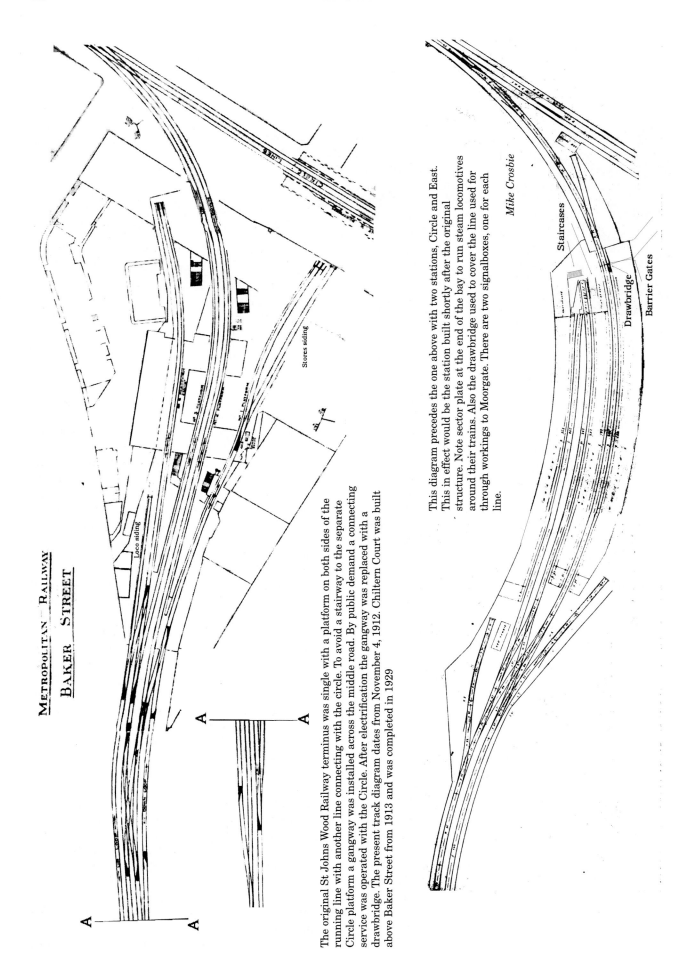

Metropolitan — Railway
Baker Street

Loco siding

Stores siding

A A

A A

The original St Johns Wood Railway terminus was single with a platform on both sides of the running line with another line connecting with the circle. To avoid a stairway to the separate Circle platform a gangway was installed across the middle road. By public demand a connecting service was operated with the Circle. After electrification the gangway was replaced with a drawbridge. The present track diagram dates from November 4, 1912. Chiltern Court was built above Baker Street from 1913 and was completed in 1929

Mike Crosbie

Staircases

Drawbridge

Barrier Gates

This diagram precedes the one above with two stations, Circle and East. This in effect would be the station built shortly after the original structure. Note sector plate at the end of the bay to run steam locomotives around their trains. Also the drawbridge used to cover the line used for through workings to Moorgate. There are two signalboxes, one for each line.

The original Kings Cross station of the undergound in 1910. A temporary sign draws attention to the fact that trains can be boarded from here direct to the Japan- British Exhibition at Olympia 'with a station right into the crowds'.

London's Transport Museum

1869 they adopted the less than satisfactory LNWR chain brake that caused some unpleasant jolting for the passengers. In 1875 simple vacuum brake was introduced, later under railway regulations this was converted to automatic vacuum brake. With the arrival of electrification the Westinghouse brake was adopted.

The Met built many four-wheel coaches with gas illumination. It had been planned originally to operate like a shuttle, with trains of three carriages comprising of 48 first class, 80 second class and 80 third class passengers with a ten minute service. From the opening it quickly became obvious that this would not suffice and on February 1, 1863 twelve express trains were provided in either direction at the busiest time of day. These expresses conveyed first and second class only. The only intermediate stop was the Edgware Road station. They took thirteen minutes to cover the entire line whereas the normal timing was 18 minutes. To compare this with the introduction of electricity later which took 12 minutes on the original section between Bishop's Road to Farringdon Street. The express trains were withdrawn on March 31, 1863.

The original timetable provided for 67 trains each way on weekdays with 48 on Sundays, with suspension during church hours. Trains stopped at all stations and took only 18 minutes for the journey of three miles sixty chains. These would be from the originally sited station at Farringdon Street.

All the trains carried 1st, 2nd, and 3rd class passengers up until December 17, 1906 when classes were abolished. Gower Street was renamed Euston Square on November 1, 1909.

With electrification, compartment carriages were superseded by saloon coaches of 53 ft length on four wheel bogies. The compartment coaches were used then on the Aylesbury extension. On June 1, 1910 Pullman cars *Mayflower* and *Galatea* were introduced in which light refreshments were served. They ran from the city and called at Met & GCR Joint stations in the countryside, eventually reaching the attenuated Verney Junction.

To describe the railway as a success would greatly understate the truth, it was incredible and carried nearly $9\frac{1}{2}$ million passengers in the first year of its existence. In the following year it carried 12 million. At the outset the board had promised to carry goods relieving the streets above. In fact there was little room for goods on the Circle. Goods yards were built on the extension out of London. But the popularity of the line to Londoners wanting to move around the city meant that the capital undertaking of goods and livestock stations could not be justified nor could much of a pathway be available, even off peak. So very little was done in that area. The one sad note to the success of the Metropolitan Railway was that its architect and driving force from the 1840's, Charles Pearson, had died in September 1862, just four months before the trains began to run.

It seemed at first that a great accord had been struck between the Great Western Railway who now had access for their trains across London and the Metropolitan Railway which had a partnership with a main supplier of rolling stock. The relationship soured however with the Met's prospective expansion to Moorgate Street. The existing line was obviously successful and prospects were good. The Met were not inclined to allow the GWR to share in the stock allocation for this new line company on the grounds that the GWR had no statutory right to further allocations than that which they had already received. Possibly the Met were not too keen on the GWR being too powerful an influence. The GWR were piqued as the new stock was selling successfully and they felt that they were entitled to share in the success and even went to law on the subject, but to no avail. They reacted with ire and tested the Met's mettle with a threat to withdraw all the rolling stock facilities on July 18, 1863 and that they would cease to work the railway at the end of September. The Met were not entirely happy with the GWR in any case as they wanted a better service other than four trains an hour with a fifteen minute service and perforce they should take matters into their own hands. The GWR were selling their shares of stock, as also was the City of London. Therefore the Met took the view that the GWR were no longer entitled to sit on the board of the Met under the Act of 1854. Fortunately the Met had a resourceful General Manger to match the hour, Sir Myles Fenton who had joined the Met as Operating Superintendent July 1, 1862. With deftness of hand he drew upon the rivalry of another company, it was always very possible to play one off against another in the mendacious world of opposing railways and the Met were forming a connection with some powerful competitors. Also the hand of John Parson never seemed to be far away in conflict with the GWR. Sir Myles appealed to the Great Northern Railway at Kings Cross and the London & North Western Railway at Euston. From both these companies he received undertakings to loan carriages. With regard to engines the Met could have been in a very difficult position as it was precluded from using conventional engines. Here destiny was at the Met's aid. Archibald Sturrock, the Locomotive Superintendent of the GNR, with a nice twist of irony, a former manager of Swindon Works, had already prepared at Doncaster a few condensing locomotives for the prospective service of the GNR for the section from Kings Cross to Farringdon Street and Moorgate from September 1 1863. Other engines he now adapted with a pipe and flexible tube leading from the exhaust pipe of the engine to the tender. The new arrangement would of course mean that for the first time the standard gauge would be used, involving the unused third rail. With use this was found defective. A lot of perspiration had to be expelled to bring the line to up to standard before the deadline.

Temporary standard gauge trains began to work from August 11 shakily at first until various problems were overcome. With help from the GNR, and the GWR in sulk, the Met pushed on with renewed confidence towards Moorgate with the Finsbury Circus Extension Act of August 6, 1861, Moorgate was reached on December 23, 1865. From October 1, 1863 the Great Northern Railway's City and Suburban service began from Kings Cross to Farringdon Street, along with the Met they continued on to Moorgate when it opened.

In terms of this alliance the arrangement with the GWR was never restored and the latter sold off share stock acquired under the agreement.

Obviously the suburban railway of London was now required to meet in the formation of a circle. To achieve this an Act for a Notting Hill & Brompton Extension received the Royal Assent on July 29, 1864. This effectively carried the railway from Paddington to South Kensington. At the same time an Act for a line from Moorgate Street to Minories, Tower Hill. This carried the circle to a 'caliper' formation with the gap from South Kensington to Tower Hill. This became the creation of the adjoining Metropolitan District Railway with spurs from South Kensington to Gloucester Road to a junction with the West London Railway at West Brompton.

The new line from Paddington to Gloucester Road was opened on October 1, 1868. It opened in sections Praed Street, Bayswater, Notting Hill Gate, High Street (Kensington) and Gloucester Road. It reached South Kensington on December 24, 1868. The new Metropolitan District Railway opened their line from South Kensington to Westminster Bridge. This line was at the outset worked by the Metropolitan until July 2, 1871. Extensions came fairly quickly, Blackfriars was reached on May 30, 1870 and the Mansion House on July 3, 1871.

In the west the District constructed its own tracks from South Kensington to Gloucester Road south side. It then ran a branch to West Brompton run by the Met. from April 12, 1869. The District also built a line from High Street Kensington to Earls Court and turning north again to join the West London Railway south of Kensington Addison Road, it became Olympia from December 19, 1946.

Through trains from Blackfriars to West Brompton began August 1, 1870, worked by the Metropolitan until July 3, 1871 when the District acquired its own stock.

The Metropolitan was also restlessly pursuing their ambitions in the east and a line

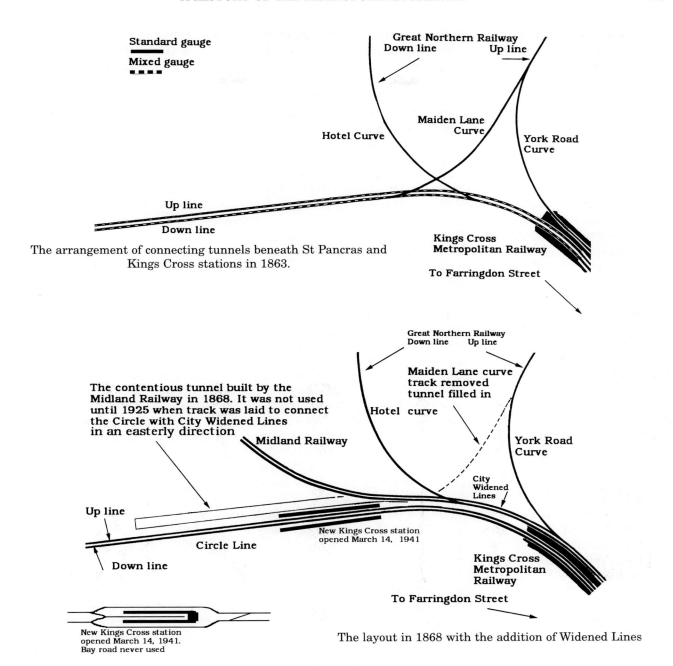

Standard gauge
Mixed gauge

Great Northern Railway
Down line   Up line

Hotel Curve

Maiden Lane
Curve

York Road
Curve

Up line

Down line

Kings Cross
Metropolitan Railway

To Farringdon Street

The arrangement of connecting tunnels beneath St Pancras and
Kings Cross stations in 1863.

The contentious tunnel built by the
Midland Railway in 1868. It was not used
until 1925 when track was laid to connect
the Circle with City Widened Lines
in an easterly direction

Midland Railway

Great Northern Railway
Down line   Up line

Maiden Lane curve
track removed
tunnel filled in

Hotel curve

York Road
Curve

Up line

City
Widened
Lines

New Kings Cross station
opened March 14, 1941

Circle Line

Down line

Kings Cross
Metropolitan
Railway

To Farringdon Street

New Kings Cross station
opened March 14, 1941.
Bay road never used

The layout in 1868 with the addition of Widened Lines

was opened to Bishopsgate, Liverpool Street from November 1, 1909, completed on July 12, 1875. From February 1, until the new station was built the Met ran into the Great Eastern Railway terminus at their own cost. John Parson maintained that the Met need reach no further than here. Obviously not a Circle man.

Rails reached Aldgate on November 18, 1876. From Aldgate to Mansion House was the joint property of the Metropolitan and Metropolitan & District Railways. The final railway of 1¼ miles was opened on October 6, 1884. The completion of the Circle had been contentious business between the Met and the Metropolitan District, the latter was born out of the need to achieve this under strong public pressure. In

order that the public's interest would be served. Independent financial interest had taken a hand with the formation of a Metropolitan Inner Circle Completion Railway Company, incorporated on August 7, 1874. Powerful interests exerted influence when a select committee was appointed by the House of Lords took a hand in these matters. They were to investigate the two circle companies and their antagonism against the completion Company. The upshot was that a further Act of August 11, 1879 virtually authorised the two railways to complete the circle. In view of the rapid progress that had been made from the first section being opened it reveals just how much quarrellous differences between individuals can negate progress. It had required statutory enforcement to drag the now conflicting railways together. The Metropolitan rushed forward its own line to Tower Hill in three nights and two days which it opened on September 25, 1882. Sir Edward Watkin, chairman of the Met, tried to spike progress of the District from his chairmanship of the South Eastern Railway. He opposed works near Cannon Street station and with the East London Railway tried to raise objections on the Whitechapel Extension. In 1883 the District obtained powers to build twelve chains of line for a terminus station at Whitechapel of its own.

The District continued building their line - Mansion House - Aldgate - Whitechapel as part of the circle. The short section from this to Aldgate was not completed until 1884.

The completion of the Circle being empowered as a Joint undertaking the Met pre-empted the District with its Aldgate-Tower Hill section. On completion of the Circle this Tower Hill station was closed on October 13, 1884 and demolished to be replaced with the Joint Tower of London station. The Joint undertaking for completion of the Circle obtained possession of the Aldgate - Tower section having to reimburse the Metropolitan for its line. The Met even tried to foist extra costs onto the District but was not sucessful. At last, the completed Circle was brought into public use on October 6, 1884. In the public interest parliament decided that the warring factions would have to be made to run in harmony and stipulated a clause to the Act that each of the two railways would, by statutory obligation, have to allow working over each other's lines. Under the agreement District trains ran anti-clockwise on the inner track. Metropolitan ran clockwise on the outer track. This palliative remained in place up until the formation of the London Passenger Transport Board in 1933.

The District built their western extension to Hammersmith and opened it on September 9, 1874. This became highly competitive by giving a more direct route to the city from Hammersmith than the earlier line of the Met from Paddington. Further, over the LSWR metals the District were able to reach Richmond by June 1, 1877.

Growing in confidence the District decided it did not feel adequately served by the erstwhile working agreement with the Metropolitan and so on January 3, 1870 it gave the Met the statutory eighteen months notice that this agreement was to be terminated. The Met had run the District lines at 55% of the gross receipts. Metropolitan directors represented on the board of the District resigned. This introduced a former adversory of Watkin, James Staats Forbes as a director. He had been

General Manager of the London Chatham & Dover Railway and was realigned with his opposer by this appointment. The District reconstituted the board with its own managing director.

It built repair works and sheds at West Brompton, now called Lillie Bridge. It ordered its own locos from Beyer Peacock, after the same design of those used on the Met. Twenty-four 4-4-0 tanks were supplied from 1871. On June 3, of the same year it began working its own services. To meet this the company also acquired its own rolling stock.

The Metropolitan found close support with the Great Northern Railway in the east of the circle and later the Midland Railway.

Kings Cross Area

When the early North Metropolitan Railway promoted a line of cut and cover from Paddington to Battle Bridge, Kings Cross they planned an arrangement of hoists and cables to connect with the GNR. The incongruity of this probably held the seeds of its failure.

An Act of July 21, 1856 authorised powers for a branch from the Metropolitan Railway to the front of the GNR terminus and a junction with the GNR near the southern entrance of a tunnel under the Regents Canal. This was intended as a single line connection and became known as the Maiden Lane curve or Western branch. This branch was intended to be in standard gauge only. Its exact purpose is not very clear but possibly the Met saw a prospect of some working arrangement with the GNR, or at least an option to do so. Not wanting to have all its eggs in the GWR basket.

The Metropolitan Railway Act of May 25, 1860 authorised the purchase of land opposite the GNR terminus. Further the Great Northern & Metropolitan Junction Railway Act of July 23 authorised a branch be constructed on the west side of the GNR station, joining the GNR line at Regents Canal tunnel mouth. With these works under construction another connection was authorised by a Metropolitan Railway Act of July 11, 1861. The second line swung eastwards from the Maiden Lane curve seventy yards north of Caledonia Street joining the Met at the junction of Grays Inn Road and Pentonville Road. This came be know as the York Road curve (York Road being the name given to Maiden Lane in 1853).

After much procrastination the upshot was that three branches were authorised at Kings Cross between the GNR and the Met. The Maiden Lane curve or Western branch, the Hotel Curve 'down line' and the York Road curve of the eastern branch 'up' into Kings Cross

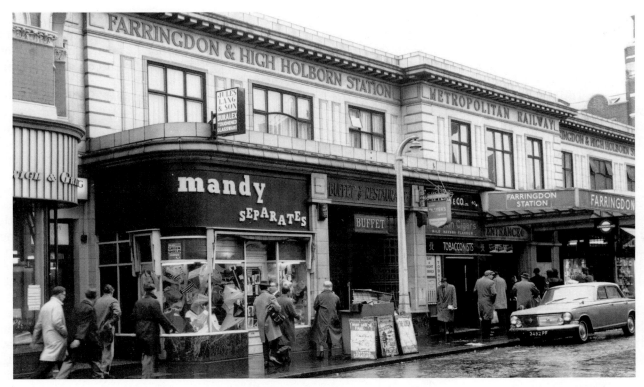

Farringdon station, rebuilt in the early twentieth century style with a frieze containing the serif lettering that would stand in contrast to the Gill style lettering to follow in the new works programme of London Transport in the thirties. A period flavour of the sixties is compounded by the newspaper billboard that announces 'Beatles London flat raided'; this view on April 24, 1964.

John Edgington

Station of the Met were all constructed in brickwork on the 'cut and cover' principle.

The Hotel Curve was completed in August 1862, before the opening of the Met main line on January 10, 1863. It is probably this link that was used to supply LNWR and GNR carriages to reach the Met after disaffection of the GWR seven months after opening.

On his inspection Colonel Yolland of the Board of Trade observed the construction was objectionable, as the junction had been constructed very close to the mouth of the tunnel and would require closely observed signal operation. The branches were both single track and on sharp curves of eight chain radius and in the case of Maiden Lane track a gradient of 1 in 46 and with 1 in 48 on Hotel Curve which being for 'down' trains would prove a testing experience for heavily loaded steam locomotives causing much slippage and stalling.

Signalling was controlled from a round house built in the centre of the triangle formed by the main line and two intersecting branch tunnels. This was regarded as being the first occasion of a complete junction and signalbox being enclosed inside a tunnel.

The facing points to the Hotel curve were operated by the Metropolitan station signalbox. A Captain Tyler of the BoT inspected the working again on September 26, 1863. He insisted that the lever in the junction roundhouse which 'slotted' the 'down' platform starting signal should also lock these points in position. The tunnel walls adjacent to these points were given wide clearance in the possible employment of pointsmen with flags at these locations to verify clearance to drivers. However from the opening day Spagnoletti block instruments were employed in conjunction with fixed signals.

On October 1, 1863 GNR suburban trains began to run to Farringdon Street. The Maiden Lane curve, western branch was described by the inspecting officer in the same context of the eastern York Road and Hotel Curve, with rails laid. Whatever the reason for the Maiden Lane curve it did not have any regular service as all GNR trains were routed to the east.

A situation of the trains from and to the south-east on the GNR reversing into Kings Cross was not a very satisfactory working arrangement so a station at York Road was constructed in 1865 and opened in February 1866, although 'down' trains continued to reverse into Kings Cross until August 1875 when a new suburban platform was introduced. On February 1, 1878 a platform known as Kings Cross suburban was opened on the Hotel Curve itself.

Intensity of use for the eastern circle was

bound to be an issue eventually and the Metropolitan foresaw this by seeking additional lines between Kings Cross and Moorgate whereby the traffic of other lines could be segregated from the Metropolitan. An act of July 11, 1861 sought powers for this further, with a Finsbury Circus Extension Act of August 6, 1861 came an additional powers Act July 25, 1864.

Part of the plan was for a short new length of tunnel to the west of the Hotel curve to realign the junction. Also a new curve to be built curving north on a rising gradient of 1 in 58 on the east side of the Midland main line beneath the prospective St Pancras station to Camden Mews. There a connection was made with the Midland London extension at St Paul's Road Junction, 1 mile 1 chain in length.

The London, Chatham & Dover Railway formed a junction with the Met at Farringdon Street on January 1, 1866 after a bridge had been built at Blackfriars across the Thames. Connection with the LCDR allowed the GNR to run a through north - south passenger service from February 20, 1866. This continued until June 30, 1908.

From July 1, 1867 all passenger services on the existing GNR connections were withdrawn and LCDR trains were reversed at Farringdon Street. The existing single line tunnels and the roundhouse signal cabin were demolished to make room for new works. The Maiden Lane tunnel was filled with spoil and the southern end bricked up with a small doorway to access a cast iron pipe carrying the Fleet Sewer at the crown of the tunnel. Apparently no longer valid for the prospective use it was intended for.

The Met had sought powers in 1865 to build a tunnel under the proposed site of St Pancras station with a view to the widened lines being extended to Praed Street Junction. The Midland successfully opposed this, in view of their own plans for under platform goods station. However the Midland undertook to build a tunnel for the Met for an annual recompense of 6 per cent on the cost of £22,188 and a rent for occupancy. It was found subsequently that the initial cost had been excessive to the cost of £872, which was an engineering requirement put in solely to accommodate support for the St Pancras station Hotel, the Met were committed to this agreement whereby they paid £52 in perpetuity. They tried to revise it but the Midland held them to the agreement. There were proposals to rent the tunnel in May 1902 for mushroom growing and again in 1909 for a rifle range but the Met preferred to keep the tunnel vacant if they could not receive an annual rent of £1,400 per annum. In 1925 the 770ft tunnel was extended 220ft to make a new

junction with the eastbound Circle Line and a single electrified track was laid to join the Widened Lines where tracks were also electrified. A fast service of Met trains from the Northern Extension was introduced, it ran from March 15, 1926 until April 27, 1935. The Metropolitan station was rebuilt further west and the east bound Circle Line moved into the old tunnel. So having been unused for 58 years, half of it was reopened in 1926, the 1868 tunnel is now used every day.

A new roundhouse was built in the space between the Midland tunnel and the realigned Hotel curve and for 57 years held the Midland Junction signalbox, this being maintained by the Metropolitan at Midland expense under an agrement of 1867 between them.

The alterations involved the redesigning of the lines at the Metropolitan Kings Cross station. The 'up' line of the GNR had a platform on each side as it made connection with the Met main line at the east end of the station. All lines were spanned by a single roof which would have to be demolished to widen the station. Consequently the northernmost platform was demolished to make room for a single track and a new platform on the north side at the east end of the original station to accommodate GNR and Midland trains. 'Down' trains used the north face of the existing island platform.

The new lines were extended to Farringdon Street in a new tunnel, this dived beneath the existing line and climbed a 1 in 40 gradient to reach the level. The line was opened to GNR traffic on February 17, 1868 with goods trains from the previous month. Midland trains first ran to Moorgate July 13, 1868 shortly before the opening of St Pancras.

Although mixed gauge had been accommodated there is no evidence that broad gauge trains ever ran over the new lines between Kings Cross and Farringdon Street. The last broad gauge train ran over the Met on March 15, 1869, the outer rail to produce the 7ft gauge was removed shortly afterwards.

The additional tracks came to be known as the 'City Widened Lines'. First section between Farringdon and Aldersgate was brought into use on March 1, 1866. Between Aldersgate and Moorgate on July 1, 1866. Both routes joined with the lines at Kings Cross and St Pancras by January 17, 1868

On June 20, 1892 a subway was opened between the Met station and the GNR terminus forecourt.

An additional short extension line was built and opened on December 15, 1906 to connect with the new Piccadilly & Brompton railway. All remained as it was until the opening of the new Kings Cross Met station in 1941.

Interior of Farringdon behind the steam locomotive no L46 on September 22 1957. Just outside the station cover is the signalbox. Evidently, from the poster, the England football team are to play Bulgaria.

H C Casserley

Not to be left out the LNWR began running a service from its ally the North London Railway terminus of Broad Street over the North London line and West London Railway to Earls Court and Mansion House over the District, they had contributed to the cost of Mansion House station. To run this they used the Webb compound tanks fitted with condensing pipes.

On September 1 1905 steam was replaced with electric traction on the Inner Circle. Some GWR goods trains still continued to Smithfield. Steam was replaced on the H&C in 1906.

At the time of writing much development is

The Widened Lines passing beneath the Circle prior to Farringdon station over Ray Street gridiron.

Bill Simpson

Very prevalent steam on the underground at Aldgate station with 'A' class tanks, note the earlier practice of numbering the engines on their chimneys. The Inner Circle engine on the right is taking the opportunity to exhaust before the tunnel sections to come. A fine display of semaphores recalls the earlier practice before electrification, that was hastened in with greater vigour than on the conventional country lines. The lines off to the left are those to Aldgate East, Whitechapel and New Cross. The train on the left foreground is for Addison Road over the Hammersmith & City line. As it is prior to electrification this scene must be before 1905 Originally the through tracks to Tower Hill were in the centre, possibly after electrification, the through lines were moved to the outside.

London Underground Railway Society

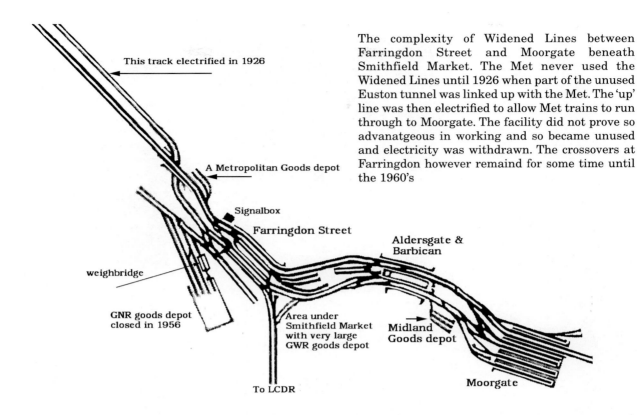

This track electrified in 1926

A Metropolitan Goods depot

Signalbox

Farringdon Street

weighbridge

GNR goods depot
closed in 1956

Area under
Smithfield Market
with very large
GWR goods depot

To LCDR

Aldersgate &
Barbican

Midland
Goods depot

Moorgate

The complexity of Widened Lines between Farringdon Street and Moorgate beneath Smithfield Market. The Met never used the Widened Lines until 1926 when part of the unused Euston tunnel was linked up with the Met. The 'up' line was then electrified to allow Met trains to run through to Moorgate. The facility did not prove so advanatgeous in working and so became unused and electricity was withdrawn. The crossovers at Farringdon however remaind for some time until the 1960's

taking place at Kings Cross the platforms enclosing the Hotel Curve have been removed and all evidence of it. York Road station has gone, the platforms removed and the tunnel mouth looks darkly derelict. The 'Thameslink' service from Bedford to Brighton uses the Midland tunnel link and Widened Lines but is no longer connected to the London Transport lines.

Grandly mid Victorian, the new Kensington station on its completion in 1868. Later the name was changed to High Street Kensington to avoid confusion with South Kensington.

Railway Gazette

Edgware Road station circa 1905 showing the original steam shed. An A class is passing with a Hammersmith & City train one of the early electric trains. Towering in the distance is a new building to the London skyline, the Great Central Hotel at Marylebone. Alterations to the Marylebone Road on the left and the construction of the London Transport building where the shed stands has made this view totally unrelateable to the present, only the hotel building remains as such.

National Railway Museum, LPC Collection

Baker Street platform 1 looking north, this platform ends at buffer stops, whilst platforms 2 and 3 continue to Aldgate.
London Underground Society

MetroVick electric loco no 5 'John Lyon' evidently destined at some time for WembleyPark. It is seen here on lines at Bakr St prior to World War Two. The signalbox is remarkably unlike the design of most Met signlboxes. Note that the loco is on a siding on the other side of the platform line.

Moorgate on June 23, 1961 with a Metrovick hauled train bound for Chesham hauled by no 12 'Sarah Siddons'. A long standing connection with the Great Northern survives with diesel locomotives, they would have little difficulty with the 1 in 40 climb at Farringdon. All of this area is of course now built over with the Barbican complex that began shortly after this date.

H C Casserley

Perhaps in view of its close proximity to the City of London the station at Moorgate was given greater architectural significance with this classical frontage. It was not so much respected by German bombers as this was all that remained on June 23, 1955. The entire area was reconstructed with the Barbican development of the sixties, the station being very much a part of this.

H C Casserley

Engine no 11 'George Romney' at Moorgate, remarkable to see a water column still remaining so long after electrification, this would have been for the use of Great Northern and Midland, later LNER steam locos. This view on June 23, 1961. The building behind is Moorgate substation

H C Casserley

A remarkable photograph of Moorgate on June 23, 1945, the serious results of bomb damage are clearly evident. Unscathed on its brick plinth is an original City & South London Electric Locomotive no 56. Behind is early electric stock train of the former Metropolitan railway

H C Casserley

Aldersgate station on November 13, 1954. The signalbox stands on the centre platform between the lines for Blackfriars and Kings cross in the foreground and the Circle line upon which a Met train is standing. Note the electric lights, Aldersgate station was the first to be installed with these in 1880 which were a considerable improvement on the gaslights. This view on November 13, 1954, the station was renamed Aldersgate & Barbican, now just Barbican.

London Underground Railway Society

Notting Hill Gate in the 1960's

London Underground Railway Society

Kensington station shortly after being completed in 1868, with delicate spherical gasoliers. It was later called High Street, note the contractors saddle tank locomotive.

Railway Gazette

MetroVick electric loco no 14 'Benjamin Disraeli' waits to depart from Liverpool Street on June 11, 1961 with a train for Aylesbury. Note the distinctive round topped doors of Met stock open on the right, supposed to give clearance in tunnels.

H C Casserley

Baker Street before the restorative work of 1983. The skylights are covered and striplighting illuminates forcefully compared to the present soft atmospheric quality. The restoration was so well done that a victorian dress or even the odd deerstalker hat would not look out of place!

London Underground Railway Society

Sunday in South Kensington in the mid-1960's. This station did not have the restoration work of other stations and is therefore original to its 1860's construction. This is apparent in the deteriorating condition of the entrance.

London Underground Railway Society

Cut and cover chaos, a section where the line will pass from the open to a tunnel.

Railway Gazette

Construction uderway in the early 1860's, probably near Kings Cross area.

Railway Gazette

Meeting of different electric motive power at Liverpool Street, the multiple unit, O or P stock and the locomotive no 16 'Oliver Goldsmith'. with 'Liverpool Street' on the front so this will have arrived from the extension lines north. The unit is en route for Whitechapel.

D M Hibbert / London Underground Society

Electric locomotive no 2 'Oliver Cromwell' leaving Baker St for Aylesbury in the 1930's. Note the signalbox, as seen on page 31. It is obviously being demolished or altered to allow construction of the building behind.

London's Transport Museum

The original Aldgate station of the Metropolitan Railway. Dating of photographs precisely can be difficult but on this print clues are evident. The hording on the newspaper stand refers to 'Pit Disaster' in terms of an explosion. This is almost certainly the terrible explosion at Pretoria Colliery near Westhoughton in Lancashire on December 21, 1910 when 344 men and boys were killed. Some confirmation of this is followed by the reference to the 'Exhibition' board top left, this would be the Japan-British-Exhibition of 1910 at Shepherds Bush.

London's Transport Museum

A very different building front at Aldgate on June 8, 1975. This neo-Venetian styling by C W Clark prevailed as a style developed by him on Metropolitan stations rebuilt throughout the early years of the twentieth century, before the first world war stopped the work. This continued after the war into the 1920's when Chiltern Court was completed.

John Edgington

London has a justifiable reputation as a city with an
abundance of oddities and the arrival of the Metropolitan
Railway has added to its store. Here is 23-24 Leinster
Gardens. a facade structure built to conform the building
line, its real purpose was to conceal the railway. A popular
joke in London was to send people to this 'dwelling', seen
here on November 11, 1965.

John Edgington

TOP RIGHT Rear of Leinster Gardens, the depth from front
to back is only 5 ft.

Railway Gazette

RIGHT The area of Leinster Gardens with pioneer
excavations in the early 1860's, which gives a good indication
of the earliest scenes on the building of the Inner Circle.

Railway Gazette

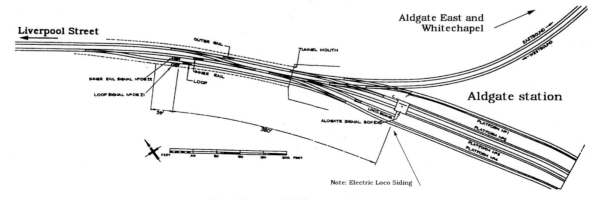

Track layout of Aldgate station

Mike Crosbie Collection

A view up the Ladbroke Grove Road beneath the elevated H&C which extols its connections particularly for the GWR. Eventually to avoid confusion on the Met the company made this Ladbroke Grove station, to distinguish it from Notting Hill Gate on the Inner Circle. The H&C belies the name 'Underground' as it is all very much overground.

London Underground Railway Society

Chapter Two

The HAMMERSMITH & CITY Railway

The borough of Hammersmith apparently had a strong sense of identity and access to greater prospects for the Metropolitan. Yet it felt left out by railway development close by, the North London Railway (1851) professed to serve the district with a Hammersmith & Chiswick station to the west. This was served by a branch line from Acton Gate junction. From the eventual site of the H&C station to the former was some distance and on reaching it the train would then take the traveller destined for east London some twenty miles round the north of London, an excess of time and money. The Hammersmith & Chiswick station in fact closed to passengers from January 1, 1917. The Hammersmith & City Company formed the first branch from the Met with the Hammersmith & City Railway which was a separate company. This was incorporated by an Act of July 22, 1861 to build a branch of 2¼ miles in mixed gauge from Green Lane Junction, this later became the now familiar Westbourne Park station, to a terminus near Hammersmith Broadway.

Capital was authorised at £180,000 in £10 shares. Working arrangements were made with the GWR and the Metropolitan and it was opened on June 13, 1864, virtually eighteen months after the opening of the first section of the Inner Circle. The first section of this ran over the GWR from Bishop's Road to Westbourne Park. It continued to serve the interests of the GWR and Met even though it ran as an independent concern.

Hammersmith was at the time of the early 1860's a parish of some 24,500 souls. Certainly if the Metropolitan looked to feeder branches to enrich its original capital undertaking the H&C was a good case.

The new line of just over two miles long, impressively 3000 yards of it was elevated above the streets on a viaduct, with a maximum height of 20ft, which must have been a very imposing feature in the London of 1864. This extended from the GWR at Green Lane bridge (Westbourne Park) to the original station of the Hammersmith and City. There were

41

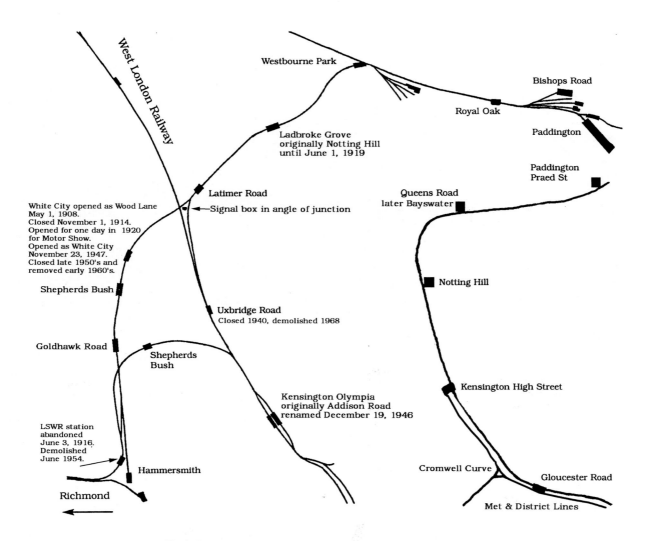

West London Railway

Westbourne Park

Bishops Road

Royal Oak

Paddington

Ladbroke Grove
originally Notting Hill
until June 1, 1919

Paddington
Praed St

Latimer Road
Signal box in angle of junction

Queens Road
later Bayswater

White City opened as Wood Lane
May 1, 1908.
Closed November 1, 1914.
Opened for one day in 1920
for Motor Show.
Opened as White City
November 23, 1947.
Closed late 1950's and
removed early 1960's.

Shepherds Bush

Notting Hill

Uxbridge Road
Closed 1940, demolished 1968

Goldhawk Road

Shepherds
Bush

Kensington High Street

Kensington Olympia
originally Addison Road
renamed December 19, 1946

LSWR station
abandoned
June 3, 1916.
Demolished
June 1954.

Hammersmith

Cromwell Curve

Gloucester Road

Richmond

Met & District Lines

Early lines and connections on the Hammersmith & City Railway.

intermediate stations at Notting Hill and Shepherds Bush (old station), these were very basic structures. The original station at Hammersmith stood on a site a few hundred feet to the north of the present one. This had station buildings fronting onto the Dartmouth Road, now Glenthorne Road.

A thirty-nine chain branch was opened from Latimer Road to connect with the West London Railway at Uxbridge Road, this was opened on July 1, 1864. This provided a link with the railways of south London. It was removed in 1940 after bomb damage. Its value having much diminished as a Middle Circle service. The GWR had used it to run over the H&C from Moorgate to Addison Road (Olympia). During its existence this branch was part of the Middle Circle.

The reason for a very modest station at Hammersmith was that plans were in hand for an extension to Richmond and the H&C ambitiously presented their own Bill in 1864 to build this. A project in which they were competed against by a rival of no small consideration, the London & South Western

Railway. They proposed to use the Addison Road station for a line to go through Hammersmith and on to Richmond. Although parliament gave the day to the L&SWR they did sanction running powers to the H&C.

In character with the now familiar mode of feeders to advancing rail heads, new bus services were established from Hammersmith to run to Turnham Green, Kew and Richmond to develop traffic for the railway as it was built. Over this line the District Railway acquired running powers.

After the opening the first services to Hammersmith were worked from Farringdon Street by the GWR on the broad gauge, at half hourly intervals, also to Addison Road. Through coaches to Addison Road were attached or detached at the Latimer Road junction. With the disaffection of the GWR the Met took over full control with standard gauge trains. The distance of running was extended to Aldersgate March 1866 and Moorgate July 1866.

The Hammersmith & City having fulfilled its role of bringing the railway to the district

Imposing Metropolitan and GWR Joint at Westbourne Park, junction station for the Hammersmith & City line, early in the twentieth century.

London Underground Railway Society

was transferred by indenture to become the joint property of the GWR and Metropolitan on July 13, 1867. An agreement was made between the GWR and Met in August 1868 for the removal of the broad gauge rails between Latimer Road and Hammersmith, just over a mile, which since March 1865 had been used only for the occasional coal train. The broad gauge on the remainder of the H&C was removed after July 1, 1869. It was also agreed that the GWR would work its traffic over the Met exclusively on the standard gauge from March 1, 1869. Perforce the GWR would be turning much of their locomotive and stock construction over to standard gauge as the prospects for the broad gauge at large were diminishing. Broad gauge trains ran to Moorgate Street until March 15, 1869 when the broad gauge was also closed between Westbourne Park and Uxbridge Road.

Shortly after opening a station was built at what is now Westbourne Park on February 1, 1866. It was modified to serve the GWR lines on November 1, 1871. Public persuasion came into play to impress upon the railway the need for a station at the junction with the West London Railway near Norland Road where Uxbridge Road station was opened on November 1, 1869. A station was built at the junction called Latimer Road on December 16, 1868.

The line of the LSWR from Addison Road to Richmond was brought into use on January 1,

1869. The construction of this line disturbed the the Hammersmith station of the H&C which meant that it was rebuilt a few hundred yards further south and opened on December 1, 1868. By this time the broad gauge tracks had been abandoned and therefore the new station was built on standard gauge only. A junction was made between the H&C and the LSWR north of Hammersmith station and after inspection by Board of Trade Inspector was brought into use on June 1, 1870. Immediately the GWR began an hourly service from Bishop's Road to Richmond exercising their joint working agreement with the H&C, with powers to run over five miles of the LSWR line to Richmond. In view of the relationship that developed between the LSWR and the GWR this was probably less than warmly received by the former. The station for Hammersmith (LSWR) was situated on a sharply curving viaduct and connected with the terminus station of the H&C by a covered way. The GWR ran their trains in this way for a few months until October 31, 1870. The Met showed some interest in the junction and ran some of its own trains from October 1, 1877 on a route from Aldgate to Richmond.

The GWR returned to maintain this service again from January 1, 1894 when they were providing half of the number trains between Hammersmith and Aldgate on ten minute intervals. They began to run an hourly service

The curved platforms of Westbourne Park on June 13, 1971. This type of station of the early underground with roof canopies supported by trusses beams and cast iron columns was swept away at some stations like Harrow with the new works programme of the thirties; here at Westbourne Park it remains still.

London Underground Society

Railway enthusiast specials abounded in the leisurely pace of forty years ago, modern times make them more difficult to organise. Here on September 9, 1957 a Stephenson Locomotive Society special hauled by MetroVick no 16 'Oliver Goldsmith' calls at the terminus at Hammersmith.

RAS Marketing

to Richmond from Aldgate. This continued until December 31, 1906 when electrification took over

In 1864 the GWR were involved in drawing up plans for a reorganisation of their system. The plans first of all involved building a new locomotive and carriage works at Oxford. This was not successful however and the eventual site decided upon was at Swindon. This also absorbed the former Wagon repair shops at Worcester that had burnt down. It also involved removal of works at Paddington leaving space to widen their lines leading into Paddington. This involved the section that was used by the

Hammersmith & City terminus in 1905.

Met and H&C. Alteration work was authorised in July 5, 1865, and the widened lines were brought into use on November 1, 1871. An underpass was constructed to carry the lines of the H&C beneath the GWR main lines and this provision was made available to trains on May 12, 1878.

The junction at Grove Road was removed in November 1914.

The Met obtained an Act in 1902 for installing electricity on the H&C. By November 5, 1906 some of the joint trains began to be worked by electricity to Hammersmith and Addison Road from December 3. Power was obtained from a new generating station built by the GWR at Park Royal completed in the summer of 1906. The plant also supplied power for lighting Paddington station replacing the Westbourne Park lighting plant of 1884 which closed on February 3, 1907 as the site was

On this view the original signalbox is visible beyond its replacement. further still are the station sidings.

H C Casserley

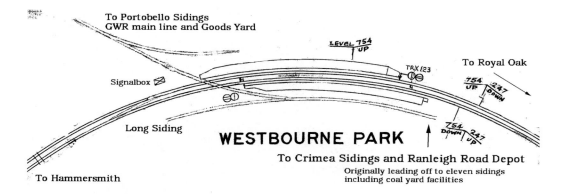

Layout of lines at Westbourne Park station.

Mike Crosbie Collection

required for further widening of the GWR main line.

Exhibition traffic for White City brought about a new station, Wood Lane, on May 1, 1908 for the opening of the White City Exhibition on May 14. This station was not used for regular traffic. When the White City ceased to be a place for exhibitions the station had no further use and was closed on October 31, 1914. It remained in service for the occasional use but was finally given the name White City on November 23, 1947. It closed totally on October 25, 1959 as a result of one of the platforms being damaged by fire. The remainder of the station was demolished in 1961. The original Shepherds Bush station was closed on March 31, 1914 and was replaced the following day with a new station at Shepherds Bush on the Uxbridge Road, on the Central Line. The private approach road to the old station now accommodates Shepherds Bush street market. Goldhawk Road station was opened in 1914.

The Met and GWR each contributed ten six-car trains of Joint stock to work the new electric trains which from April 2, 1907 this allowed the service to be extended from six to twelve trains per hour. From February 9, 1914 four hourly trains ran through to New Cross to SECR and LBSCR stations.

The Met continued to New Cross (SECR) over the East London Railway to Hammersmith with steam traction until December 2, 1906. The following day electric traction began using Met & GWR Joint stock between Hammersmith and Whitechapel up until formation of LT. They continued until November 20, 1939. The name 'Hammersmith & City' continues to be used for the line as it has for 138 years.

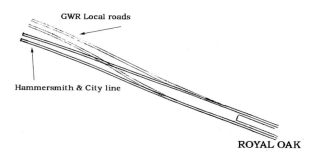

Original junction of the GWR and Hammersmith & City Railway at Royal Oak

Mike Crosbie Collection

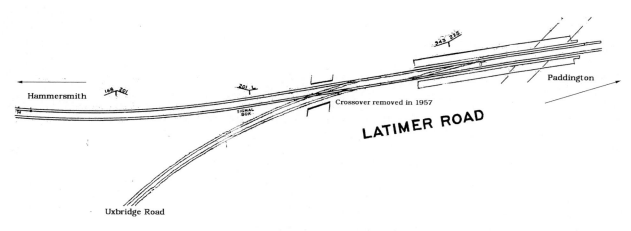

Latimer Road where the junction existed for the connecting line to Uxbridge Road and Addison Road, that became Kensington Olympia. A line much used for a long time for exhibition traffic.

Mike Crosbie Collection

Chapter Three

CONFLICT and CONFIDANTS

Conflicting interests in railway politics was rife from the days of the gauge war in the 1840's, until things began to settle down by the end of the century. The building of the Great Central Railway being the last great territorial statement that came in the 1890's. The leaders of all the private railways became like generals of their own railway army, jealously occupying a part of the kingdom, or trying to dominate it.

The personal egotism and attitude, overriding business sense, between Sir Edward Watkin Chairman of the Metropolitan Railway with his aide John Bell, secretary of 1872, and James Staats Forbes of the District Railway is well documented as prime example of destructive enmity.

Sir Edward Watkin was involved with railways from the early days and proved an imaginative and ubiquitous character. He was involved with the early days of the London & Birmingham and when the Buckinghamshire Railway was being constructed Watkin surfaces as secretary to the General Manager, of the newly formed London & North Western Railway, the notorious Captain Mark Huish. That was in 1850, he resigned from that position in 1853.

He then reappears again in the affairs of the Manchester, Sheffield and Lincolnshire Railway. First as General Manager, then becoming Chairman in 1864, where he was vociferous in the company's quarrel with his former company, the LNWR, at Manchester. He was knighted in 1868 and became a baronet in 1880.

A restless and energetic man he then became Chairman of the South Eastern & Chatham Railway in 1866 and later MP for Hythe in 1874. As a Mancunian, he remained living in Manchester.

As Chairman of the South Eastern & Chatham he advocated building a tunnel under Baker Street to connect the Met with this railway.

He became Chairman of the Metropolitan Railway on August 7, 1872 where he remained

Features of great resolve, the energetic Lancastrian Sir Edward Watkin chairman of the South Eastern & Chatham Railway; Manchester Sheffield & Lincolnshire Railway and Metropolitan Railway. He dreamed that one day there would be a railway under the English Channel.

National Railway Museum

until 1894 when he retired. His dreams took flight with the extension of the MS&L from their trans-pennine line at Annesley to London.

Watkin was also Chairman of the Channel Tunnel Company (Railway) for which an Act had been passed in both countries. An experimental tunnel was bored for 2000 yards on each side of the channel. The M&SL extension was therefore built to a continental loading gauge. The tunnel railway to the continent remained a dream until long after Watkin's death. Tragically his main line to the north, so grandly acclaimed striding the Chilterns and the midland counties finally withered from 1966. Some thirty years later, its planned under sea section became a reality and opened in 1994.

He was also the initiator of an ill fated tower promotion at Wembley Park. He bought Wembley Park for £32,929 in 1889 and formed the Tower Construction Co Ltd. His plan was for a centre with a tower not only higher than the famed construction by Eiffel in Paris, but to build on it and beneath it, restaurants, theatres, dance halls, shops turkish bath and exhibition halls. In that sense Watkin was a true visionary who conceived of a plan for what we now call a leisure complex. The first level of the Tower opened to the public in 1896. Although the railway was nearby, Met and GCR the public interest could not be drawn from the capital and a scheme of public subscription showed no promise. Vistors dwindled and the Tower began to fall derelict, ignominoiusly for Watkin as it came to be called, 'Watkin's Folly'. It was finally demolished in 1907. It did however retain the focus of Wembley Park as a sporting venue and it was ideal for the British Empire Exhibition of 1924-25 with the triumphant edifice of the new Wembley stadium. The rest is history.

Returning to railway matters, the GCR formed a Joint Committee with the Metropolitan joining it at their Quainton Road Station and leaving at Harrow South Junction. Watkin became Chairman of the Joint undertaking. He was very much the man of the Met extension and envisioned the developments alongside the line through the Chilterns. He carried the railway to Chesham and devised the absorption of a very rickety affair called the Aylesbury & Buckingham Railway opened from Aylesbury to Verney Junction in 1868. The section from Quainton Road to Aylesbury became a small part of his grand plan. He then

Ascendant Great Central Railway, the supremly impressive Robinson 'Atlantic' heads south through Waddesdon Road station early in the twentieth century

Bill George Collection

talked of a line from Verney Junction to Towcester.

By extension of the Met, up until his retirement from the board, he doubled its passenger traffic from 44,392,000 per annum to 88,513,000. The dream of another man, Charles Pearson, had been more than vindicated after so much ridicule and rebuke. The Met was now a mighty force.

John Bell was Watkin's protege, he was appointed General Manager to succeed the resourceful Myles Fenton at the beginning of 1880. He crowned this by becoming the Chairman on May 5, 1894, as Watkin retired. He remained in this position until November 28, 1901, the year that Watkin died.

James Staats Forbes had been General Manager of the London, Chatham & Dover Railway since 1862, a rival company to the SE&CR of Watkin's control. Possibly from this position the two were cast as adversories and carried their opposition with them to the London companies.

The hostility was unremitting, the two men actually exchanged verbal insults against each other. It had been considered a natural progression that the District would eventually amalgamate with the Metropolitan and perhaps, with less flinty leaders it may well have happened. The District working arrangement with the Metropolitan of them paying them 55 percent of gross receipts on local

traffic and proportion of through traffic was not considered fortuitous to the District. It expired in July 1871 and Forbes had no wish to renew it. He wanted the interlocking train services to turn over each others lines on a mileage arrangement. The Metropolitan was not interested. The District was not going to oblige the Metropolitan, and they decided to give the Metropolitan a years notice that they wished to terminate their original working arrangement in July 1871. Later in 1874 amalgamation was given a public airing but the Metropolitan would not agree. Watkin hoped by stages that the District would fall into the Metropolitan's lap. But the District soldiered on and secured powers in 1875 to make the Hammersmith Junction Railway from Hammersmith Broadway to the Kensington (Addison Road) and the Richmond line of the LSWR at Studland Road Junction. A particular area of heated competition was the exhibition traffic of the south-west suburban area of London where both the railways worked.

Arguments and litigations continued back and forth right up to 1894 after completion of the Inner Circle; when after a stroke, Sir Edward Watkin resigned the Chairmanship of the Metropolitan. By then both railways had the serious business of alternative traction to think about.

From the time John Bell became chairman he took over control of the Met's interests on the

Metro-Cammel early electric Locomotive no 10 with the 'down' Aylesbury Pullman alongside a GCR train south of Harrow c1910.

Joint Committee with the MS&LR in its march south, a Watkin company; but John Bell was not to be taken for granted. The new century brought different demands on the railways and the Metropolitan was very much a railway of their own extension with suburban services. This brought a conflict of interests with the main line railway. The result was that the GCR sought an agreement with the GWR to give them some security to reaching their Marylebone terminus under a Joint Committee.

The GWR needed to improve its Chiltern line and build a shorter route to Birmingham, so a new alliance was born. The GCR built their line leaving the route at Ashendon Junction, whilst the GWR built their connecting line from Princes Risborough to Aynho.

An example of the kind of hostility of the railways was in a dispute over the right to occupy a siding at South Kensington station. The District left locomotives there. The Met in pique removed them. The District for their part now chained an engine to the rails. The Met sent three locomotives to haul it away and failed. This kind of confrontational antics may have amused the passengers awaiting trains. But would not be so amused by the inconvenience of blocking each others services .

Sometime partners, a Robinson Atlantic on a Rugby - Marylebone train and a Jones 4-4-4T on a Baker Street train at Aylesbury on May 2,1936.

H C Casserley

The original Metropolitan Swiss Cottage station on the Finchley Road, the building is named 'Swiss Terrace'. Two features of particular interest are the coal merchant on the extreme left with bags of coal outside the front of his shop and on the right, still part of the station building, the estate agents. The former makes the point that the Metropolitan though primarily thought of as a passenger line did carry a great deal of goods traffic, especially on the northern extension. The estate agent pointedly brings to mind the Metropolitan Railway Country Estates Limited that developed the lands alongside the northern extension and created 'Metro-Land'.

London Underground Society

Chapter Four
The EXTENSION NORTH

After the success of the first stages of the Metropolitan railway there was a revival in activity for building railways in London. Speculators were waking up to the possibilities. In 1864 there were about 250 schemes for building railways in and about the capital, around 300 miles of lines, this fevered rush was what had happened in the country at large over a decade earlier. The vast majority were thrown out by parliament save four, three to complete the inner circle and a fourth to carry the Metropolitan beyond the confines of London. Watkin's grand scheme for the trunk route from the south coast to the north. The board of the Met must have realised to some extent that London would be a developing suburbia, and promoted the railway.

The Metropolitan & St John's Wood Railway was incorporated on July 29, 1864. This was a separate company in which the Metropolitan would take a large shareholding. The first section was opened as a single line on April 13 1868. There were stations at Baker Street Junction, St Johns Wood Road, Marlborough Road and Swiss Cottage. A service was operated from Moorgate to Swiss Cottage from the opening until March 7, 1869. From that time the through running ceased as trains tended to terminate at Baker Street.

After Finchley Road station the railway emerged into the sunlit uplands of rural suburbia in north London. Difficult to imagine now, but this was open rolling countryside in the later nineteenth century.

With Sir Edward Watkin in the Chair the line steadily progressed north, opening at West Hampstead on June 30, 1879.

Energetically it went still further and opened at Willesden Green on November 24, 1879 with an intermediate station at Kilburn. It was then extended to Harrow on August 2, 1880 including a station at Neasden & Kingsbury. Remarkably this railway was still pursuing its service on single track between Baker Street and Swiss Cottage which was not doubled until 1883. To occupy the single line the

The tiny station of St John's Wood Road in Spring 1910, note part of the station let to an estate agent. Top left 'Cobbett's' cricket bats recalls the very close proximity of Lord's cricket ground for which this would be the station.

London's Transport Museum

train driver had to have the requisite token for the line. In this case the tokens were *men*. The token man for the 'down' wearing a red cap and the token man for the 'up' wearing a blue. Later, tokens were replaced with belts. Tokens were exchanged by the trains entering St Johns Wood at the same time and as the Swiss Cottage train steamed in the 'red belt' jumped off the train and slid along the platform until his progress was checked by the wall at the end. At the same time 'blue belt' did the same thing on the other platform. These antics were brought to a close after a time and the tokens, less spectacularly, became a staff .

A junction with the Midland Railway was made at Finchley Road for goods traffic only just north of Swiss Cottage on October 1, 1880.

The tiny St. John's Railway Company was totally absorbed by the Metropolitan on January 1, 1883 (Act July 3, 1882), the single track section was doubled. It had been intended at one time to extend the railway to Hampstead,

In the 1920's the station was rebuilt, including buffet and tea rooms, in the style by C W Clark, the diamond shape clock was a feature of his designs. From April 1. 1925 it was renamed St John's Wood but was poorly used outside the cricket season in which it appears in this print, in June 1933. It was renamed 'Lords on June 11, 1939 but with the Bakerloo extension to Finchley Road opening in November of the same year the station was vulnerable and wartime damage proved this as it was closed not to reopen.

London's Transport Museum

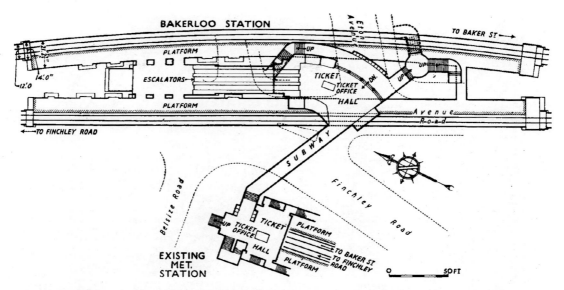

Connection between the old station and the new tube station on the Bakerloo line at Swiss Cottage.

Railway Gazette

this would have involved the line climbing a tunnel of 1 in 27. In consequence of this some very powerful 0-6-0 engines were built and were employed working traffic up until 1873 when they were sold to the Taff Vale Railway and Sirhowy Railway. The Hampstead project was completely abandoned.

The formation of a Kingsbury & Harrow Joint Committee (1874) From the Met & St Johns Rly companies carried the line on to Harrow

The locomotive running shed facilities had been situated at Edgware Road since the beginning the of the Metropolitan but after the opening of the extension another steam depot was needed. In 1880 the Neasden shed was opened where electric trains are still held to this day but that original steam shed has long since been removed. The Edgware Road shed remained until steam left the city lines.

With the incorporation of a Harrow & Rickmansworth Railway (1874) the line was extended to Pinner, opening there on May 25, 1885. Rickmansworth was reached on September 1, 1887. How the Metropolitan would have been had Watkin not been the driving force behind it, possibly it may have remained a London railway. That being said the drive north proved successfull, especially with the Metropolitan Estates department that developed the countryside alongside the extension and gave birth to the romantic suburban image of 'Metro-land'. The company promoted this artfully, publicising an image of lost utopia, the earthly roots that are deep in the heart of every city dweller. The escape beyond smog bound London to the beechwoods and rolling countryside of the Chilterns. It was an irresistible enticement and it worked.

Chorley Wood was reached in 1889. The line went on to Chalfont Road and Chesham, Amersham, Aylesbury and Verney Junction by 1894. Although the Met persisted to north Bucks as far as Verney Junction things began to thin out beyond Aylesbury and never showed any of the advantages of the nearer counties. The growth of Building Societies in the 19 century was nourishment to the realisation of home buyers

North Bucks brings into view a penurious little railway that had been promoted and eventually built by Sir Harry Verney, Bart and the Duke of Buckingham. This was between Aylesbury and Verney Junction where it made a tenuous and resisted connection to the London & North Western Railway between Oxford and Bletchley, part of the Oxford to Cambridge route. The A & B opened in 1868 and had been built very much on a shoestring conceding running rights to the GWR, almost out of pique, in the face of the LNWR's opposition. The GWR line ran from their Wycombe Railway and Maidenhead to Aylesbury via Princes Risborough. As mentioned, it seemed almost valedictory of them to support this pointless railway into Verney Junction. Although they ran only three return trains per day.

The Metropolitan Railway, spurred on by Watkin's dream, purchased the Aylesbury & Buckingham Rly, probably to its relief, as another section in the march northwards. The amalgamation took place on July 1, 1891. Consequently the Metropolitan reached Aylesbury on September 1, 1892, and with the A&B they were now over fifty miles from Baker Street.

Watkin reported in the The Times of July 19, 1899 of the cost of building the branch to

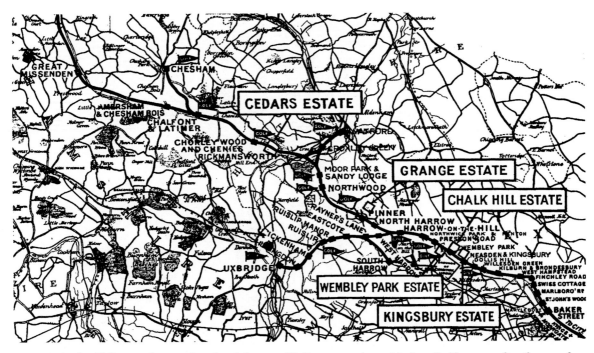

The new utopia in the Chilterns, the promise of each house with its own garden set in breathable acres after the crowds and fog of London. This was the Railway's promise with its projected image of 'Metro-Land'. Of course the commuter dream in the end defeats itself and with the intensive use of road transport the green acres were developed further and became enmeshed in a less rusticated image of suburbia.

Mike Crosbie Collection

Chesham which was £29,310. The population of Chesham at the time was 8,000. The Met secured an agreement to rebuild Verney Junction to a proper station which the LNWR entered into with the obvious requirement that the station was built to their specifications. The Metropolitan had the platform face on the south side and sidings. The entire line beyond Aylesbury was doubled in 1896.

About seven miles north of Aylesbury was the station of Quainton Road, it was here, where GCR(MS&LR) railway, with its extension to London met with its brother in arms, the Metropolitan, as planned. Watkin saw it happen from his retirement as the GCR opened its Marylebone terminus on March 15, 1899. He died two years later.

A row of Englishmens' 'castles' on Anson Road, Willesden Green.

Mike Crosbie Collection

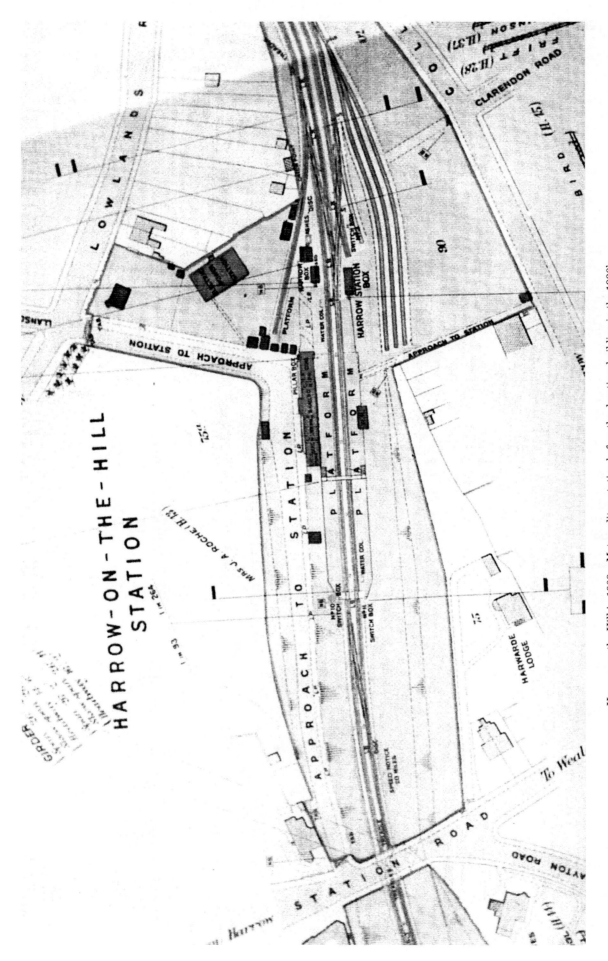

John Mock Collection

Harrow-on-the-Hill in 1908 a Metropolitan station before the drastic rebuilding in the 1930's.

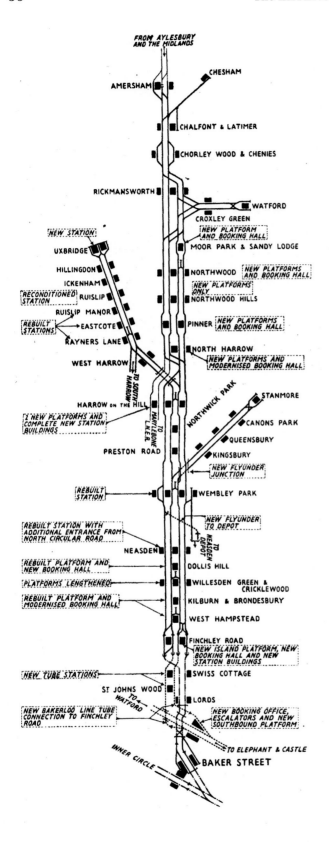

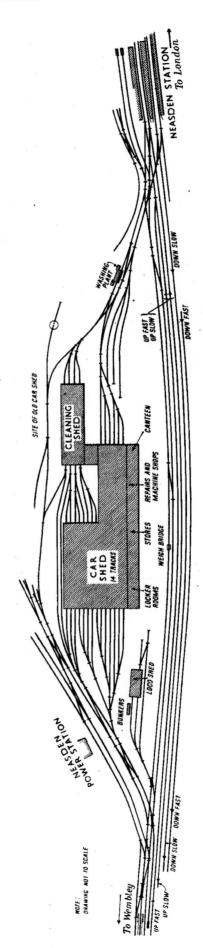

The works north to Amersham showing connections between
the Metropolitan and Bakerloo Line at Finchley Road. Also
the widening of the lines between Harrow and
Rickmansworth.

Railway Gazette

The development of Neasden up to 1945.

Railway Gazette

Metropolitan 'A' class at Willesden Green on June 4, 1904.

R K Blencowe

Willesden Green station buildings in the early sixties

London Underground Society

Willesden Green station of 1925, evidently some work is being done on C W Clark's building motif, the diamond shaped clock. The collection of small businesses and shops became part of the station milieu after the stations were rebuilt. Note the tramlines and overhead wires.

London's Transport Museum.

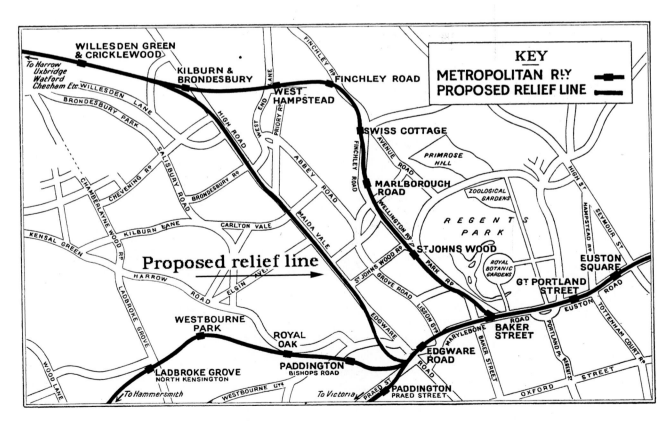

The proposed relief line that was never built. The growth of suburbia increased the demands on the north line extension. The measure eventually adopted was the extension of the Bakerloo absorbing a number of former Metropolitan stations, St John's Wood, Swiss Cottage joining alongside at Finchley Road. This eventually came to be named the present Jubilee Line.

Mike Crosbie Collection

A typical Metropolitan Railway signalbox at Willesden Green with one of the British Thomson Houston electric locomtotives no 11.

H C Casserley Collection

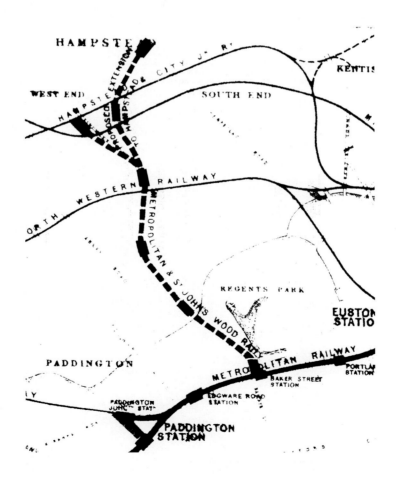

Diagram from 1865 showing the route planned of the St. John's Wood Railway and the branch to Hampstead that was subsequently abandoned.

London's Transport Museum

BAKER STREET, MARYLEBONE, RICKMANSWORTH, CHESHAM, AYLESBURY, and VERNEY JUNCTION.—Met. & G. C.

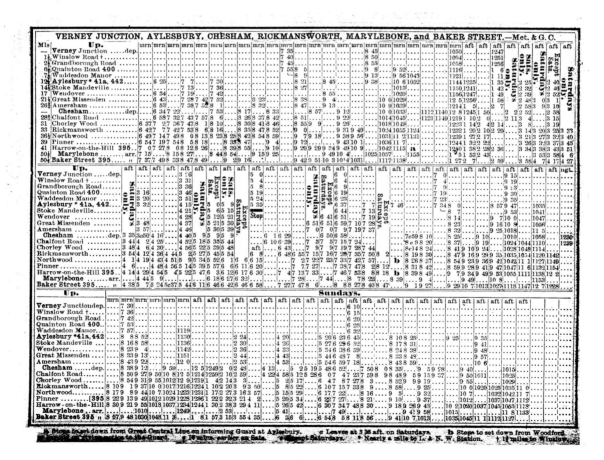

VERNEY JUNCTION, AYLESBURY, CHESHAM, RICKMANSWORTH, MARYLEBONE, and BAKER STREET.—Met. & G. C.

A timetable for the service between Baker Street and Verney Junction in 1909

Bill Simpson Collection

With the backdrop of the castellated tower of the power station at Neasden with the later steam shed and engines nos L53, L45, L50 on October 4, 1958.

R M Casserley

Metropolitan trains in the new Neasden depot.

Railway Gazette

Metro-Vick loco no 3 'Sir Ralph Verney' on a Liverpool Street to Chesham train pasing through Neasden on August 9, 1961.

John Edgington

Neasden station building is the beginning of the 'cottage style architecture of the Metropolitan, the later work of C W Clark.

London Underground Society

An up Metropolitan train crossing over the Stanmore branch line underpass junction near Wembley Park. A down Stanmore tube is departing in the foreground.

Railway Gazette

Neasden station looking towards Baker Street in the 1960's

London Underground Society

The prominent 'porthole' style driving windows on the F stock train arriving from Baker Street into Neasden bound for Rickmansworth after passing under the distinctive girder bridge carrying the former Midland line from Acton Wells Junction to Brent Junction, on August 9, 1961.

John Edgington

Set against the background of Neasden Power station the 'A' class engine no 48 photographed here on July 11, 1936. These hard working engines were being withdrawn after the closure of the Brill branch.

H C Casserley

One of the 'G' class 0-6-4T engines this one number 97 named 'Brill' on Neasden shed

H C Casserley

The car sheds at Neasden with locomotives and early electric stock in the 1950's

RAS Marketing

The later steam shed at Neasden on July 14, 1939. Tank engines L44 0-4-4T Met 'E' class and L50 0-6-2T 'F' class on the coal road with well filled bunkers, probably awaiting their turn of duty.

H C Casserley

Alongside the steam shed, the first carriage sheds for steam hauled stock at Neasden. Engine to the extreme right probably the shed pilot.

London's Transport Museum

Resplendently restored in the early sixties 'A' class engine no 23, latterly in use on the Brill branch. Here it is restored to its earliest livery and has probably been placed in position for photographs, by 'F' class 0-6-2T, now L52. Behind is the massive bulk of the power station,

London Underground Society

Two of the handsome Jones's 4-4-4 tank engines one on each side of one of the mighty 'K' class tanks preparing for another day in the Chilterns on July 11. 1936. It is regrettable that no example of these remarkable engines reached preservation.

H C Casserley

The original steam shed at Neasden that must have been replaced in the late thirties, as this view is on July 11, 1936. Engines on shed nos 112, 80, 97.

H C Casserley

LT Met and Bakerloo motormen at Neasden on photographs supplied by the late Bill Fry who can be seen bottom row second from left. And on the wartime helmeted picture below, bottom row extreme left. Numbers on units behind on top print 10099, 014083, Bakerloo 1938 tube stock and below 13262, 1938 O or P stock on Met.

Bill Fry

Wembley station in the late twenties, uncluttered by traffic.

London's Transport Museum

Snaps from the family album, another Bill Fry picture at Neasden pre World War Two with a 4-4-4 'H' class upon which he was a driver.

Bill Fry

"METRO." ROUTE TO AND FROM THE MAIN LINE RAILWAY TERMINI

Main Line Stn.	Connecting Station	Remarks
Paddington ...	Praed Street (Metro.)	Subway
	Bishop's Road (Metro.)	Covered way
Marylebone ...	Edgware Road (Metro.)	3 min. walk
	Baker Street (Metro.)	5 min. walk
Euston	Euston Square (Metro.)	5 min. walk
St. Pancras ...	King's Cross (Metro.)...	1 min. walk
King's Cross...	King's Cross (Metro.)...	Subway
Liverpool St....	Liverpool St. (Metro.)	Subway
Broad St. ...	Liverpool St. (Metro.)	1 min. walk
Fenchurch St.	Mark Lane (Metro. and District)	3 min. walk
	Aldgate (Metro.).... ...	5 min. walk
Cannon Street	Cannon Street (Metro. and District)	Subway
London Bridge	Monument (Metro. and District)	3 min. walk
St. Paul's ...	Blackfriars (District)...	Covered way
Charing Cross	Charing Cross (District)	Short walk
	Trafalgar Sq. (Bakerloo)	Short walk
Waterloo ...	Waterloo (Bakerloo) ...	Covered way
Victoria	Victoria (District) ...	Subways

The Metropolitan Railway—the World's Pioneer Underground System — provides the easiest, quickest and best route to the British Empire Exhibition. Its Train Service is unequalled for frequency and rapidity, its directness of route is unrivalled, whilst the convenience and comfort provided by the system are its outstanding features.

The "Metro" provides direct and speedy access with all parts of the Metropolis; it links up at eight points with London's Tube System, and affords an exceedingly convenient system of connection with the whole of the Main Line Termini.

A special Exhibition Station has been erected at Wembley Park, including a COVERED WAY DIRECT INTO THE EXHIBITION GROUNDS.

HOW TO GET TO AND FROM THE BRITISH EMPIRE EXHIBITION, WEMBLEY PARK.

Pre-eminently a time for the Met to play an outstanding transport role with the British Empire Exhibition that opened at Wembley on April 23 1924.

M Daniels Collection

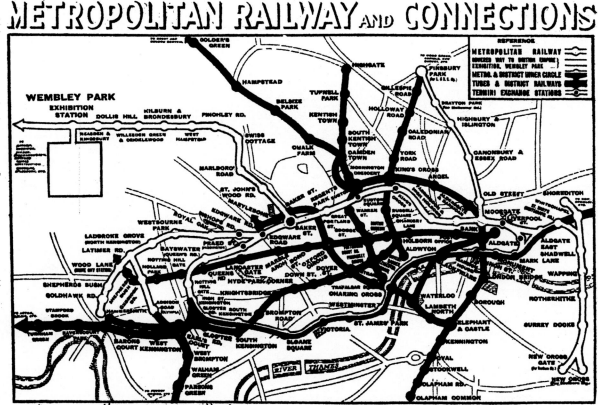

Wembley Park with an Aldgate Metropolitan line train on the far side and Bakerloo tube to Stanmore. Eventually the Bakerloo line became the Jubilee line as it is at present.

London's Transport Museum

Wembley Park in the 1960's.

London Underground Railway Society

Artist's impression of the arrangement of the burrowing junction at Harrow

Mike Crosbie Collection

Entrance to the Uxbridge station, the white building in the distance is the signalbox, with sidings on the left. This is a special working train as there are no run-round facilities at the station. The photograph is taken from the York Road overbridge

London Underground Railway Society

The original Metropolitan station at Harrow-on-the-Hill in September 1933 west side, the design was favourably received as in keeping with the town. New works in the thirties would see this robust design in brick with a classical portico entrance swept aside by Charles Holden's modern style, remaining to this day.

London's Transport Museum

Some novelty of advancing electrification at Harrow with the introduction of the new electric locos by BTH with a Chesham train seen here.

London Underground Railway Society

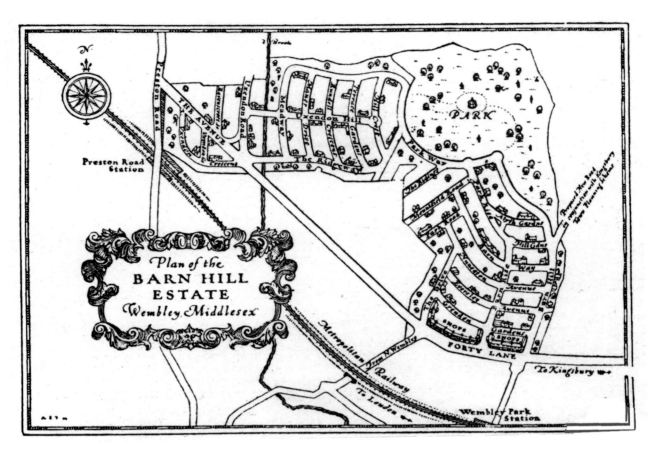

Ideal location, the Barn Hill estate at Wembley arranged between two stations.

Mike Crosbie Collection

New works at Harrow in the late 1930's brought long platforms with curved end station buildings including glazing and canopies. The platform area divested of columns to allow clear ways for mass movement and the long horizontals and verticals breaking dramatically away from former ornamentation. Harrow station was completely rebuilt with three island platforms and new station buildings on the bridge. The LNER had one of these platforms for steam workings. This view is looking north with platforms left to right 1 to 6.

Bill Simpson

The site of Watkin's Tower, Wembley stadium, which has now been demolished.

Bill Simpson

Electric unit train of 1921 stock for Uxbridge entering unreconstructed Harrow in 1925.

London Underground Railway Society

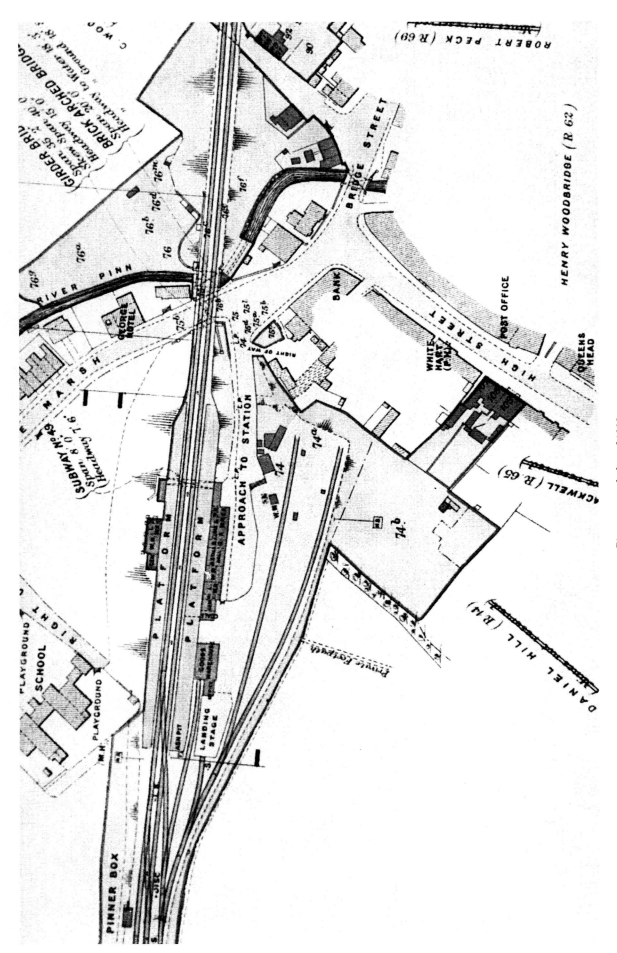

Pinner ground plan of 1908.

John Mock Collection

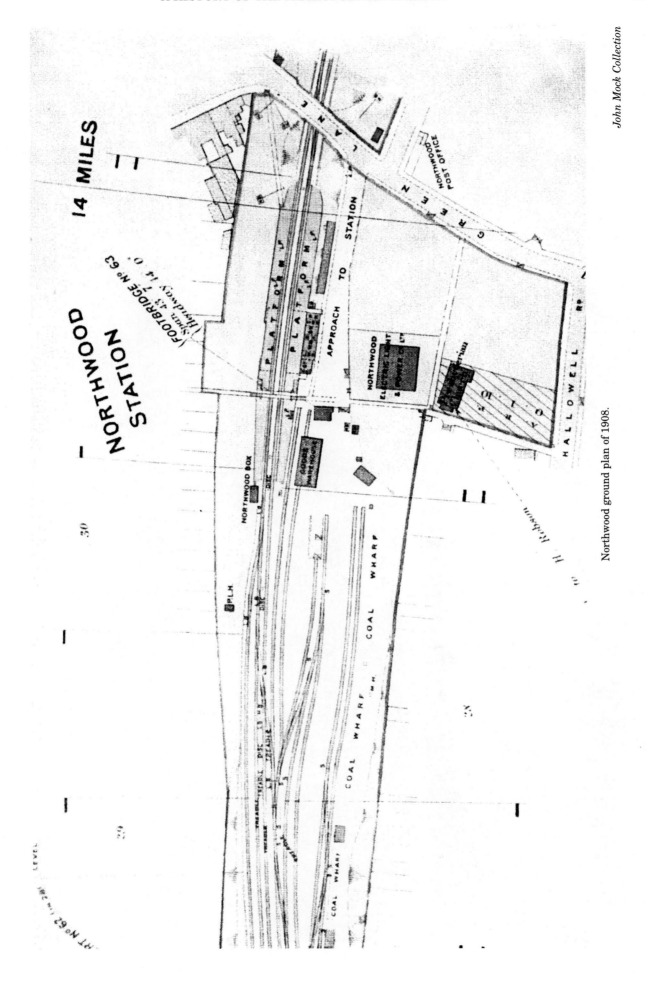

Northwood ground plan of 1908.

London Underground Society

One of the Metro-Cammel electric locomotives at Harrow shortly after electrification.

One of the former Met 'E' class on stand by duty at Rickmansworth on August 12, 1951

John H Meredith

In 1937 London Transport published plans of their intention to relieve the bottleneck of Finchley Road, a distance of two miles from Baker Street. At that time the line between those two points was simply double track. At Finchley Road they became four, but the double track section was a severe restriction and made it difficult to provide service to the intermediate stations along its length. In consequence it was planned to throw off a branch from the existing Bakerloo Line at Baker Street operating independently and calling at new stations built for Swiss Cottage and St Johns Wood, there was a plan to have a third replacing the old Marlborough Road station, to be called Acacia Road, but this was not built.

The plan also needed a rearrangement of tracks north of Finchley Road with the 'down' local 'up' local and 'down' fast and 'up' fast. This required a new 'up' platform at Finchley Road and moving platforms at West Hampstead, Dollis Hill and Kilburn. Wembley Park required further extensive alterations to accommodate the stadium traffic. Two additional lines were provided at Harrow station with the 'up' local and 'down' being converted into island platforms. Quadrupling was also planned to be carried to Rickmansworth.

The rebuilding of stations also brought the new dynamic 'London Transport' look, replacing hard worked and jaded station buildings with new column free, curved canopies and matching platform buildings with curved ends and metal window frames and glazing.

The section between Rickmansworth and Amersham had to wait until after the war in the early 1960's when the largest bridge on the Metropolitan was placed across the Rickmansworth to Pinner Road between Northwood and Northwood Hills. This lattice girder construction was the result of increasing traffic on the road beneath which was only 25ft wide at this place. The bridge on a skew angle enabled the road to be 60ft a considerable improvement required by the West Middlesex County Council.

At Kings Cross a new ticket hall was constructed for Northern, Piccadilly and Met lines, with pedestrian access to the main line stations. Note the bay on the new Met station, this was sealed off and has never been used, although it still exists. The Widened Lines were still accommodated in the rebuilding structure. The illustration gives a good account of the tremendous engineering challenges successfully undertaken by LT engineers and this only a fraction of the system!

Courtesy of the Daily Telegraph

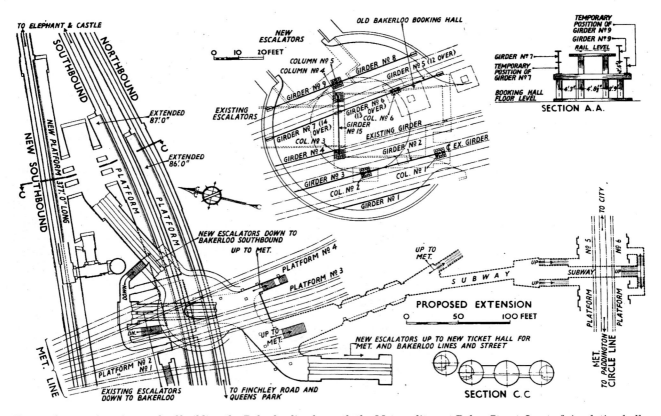

Tremendous engineering work of building the Bakerloo line beneath the Metropolitan at Baker Street. Inset of circulating hall area of Bakerloo with supporting columns.

Railway Gazette

O or P stock train on the Uxbridge branch entering Ickenham.

Colour Rail LT140

Paddington Praed Street, this view clearly shows the nature of the first underground railway as sub-surface rather than true underground as the later tube.

Bill Simpson

Busy wintery days at Rickmansworth in the late fifties with goods yard and shed extant. The MetroVicks having brought trains from the city await to return.

G H Hunt / Colour Rail LT195

Heavily engineered the short Watford branch crosses the River Gade and the Grand Union canal. Canals now so popular for leisure by contrast to their one time very hard working role. Passing over is a train of A60/62 stock in September 2002.

Bill Simpson

Through workings continue at the once independent Hammersmith & City line terminus.

Bill Simpson

Once a modest country Halt in 1906 but with population increase along the line this LPTB thirties style became very much the fully developed station at Eastcote.

Bill Simpson

Moor Park and Sandy Lodge in the late 1950's with train entering from the City. On the right are alterations taking place for the widening to accommodate four-tracks when the station was completely rebuilt to be brought into use September 9, 1961.

Colour RailLT37

An 'F" class burnished with a workworn gleam in the sunlight at Neasden.

Colour Rail LT24

Watford station with 'T' stock.

Chris Gammell / Colour Rail LT233

The new order of the 30's. The Charles Holden design of the new St Johns on the Bakerloo is a period gem with the original uplighters on the escalators.

Bill Simpson

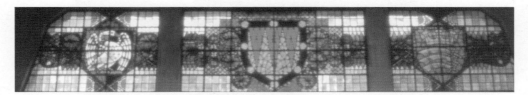

It is to be applauded that Sir Frank Pick, sought to express a new age with work by contemporary artists. Here county crests of Middlesex, Hertfordshire and Buckinghamshire are splendidly presented at Uxbridge station, the work of Erwin Bossanyi.

Bill Simpson

An 'A' class tank no L45 still with condensing pipes no longer in use prior to restoration as no 23.

Colour RailLT1

A train of 'T' stock entering Pinner.

The late Ray Oakley/Colour Rail LT275

A combination to stir nostalgia for the commonplace, with 'E' class L46 and former Met four wheel goods brake van at Croxley Tip Sidings. Below, the siding close to the junction of the Watford branch in the early seventies

L V Reason / Colour Rail / LT2; below Mike Crosbie39

METRO-LAND

PRICE TWO-PENCE

The Metropolitan Railway produced a number of high quality publications promoting the image of Metro-Land.
This one from 1926.

Mike Crosbie Collection

One of the 'H' class tank engines no 110 at Rickmansworth on August 17, 1935.

H C Casserley

Rickmansworth

This first volume ends at Rickmansworth, the place where the Metropolitan had carried their electrification from Harrow on January 5, 1925. So for thirty-five years it became the terminus for electrified working from Baker Street.

Steam engines took over trains going north, that is until the extension of electrification to Amersham and Chesham in September 1960.

The station, is situated on a considerable curve, by contrast with other stations on the northern lines. Here the transfer of traction was like a ritual dance, with locomotives of both types awaiting in sidings to move trains onward. The dexterity of this became quite a local railway feature, being accomplished with practised skill in under five minutes.

Not surprisingly the Met built a huge water tank house and water storage tank on the 'up' platform which remains to this day. A monument to those once busy days of steam when engines rushed about the station. Trains now pass it by, efficiently, but less divertingly.

A few years later, on January 3, 1959 steam was entering its twilight, it had less than a decade to survive at large. Here it it is represented by a Stanier 2-6-4 tank. They ran the service with this 'set' between Liverpool Street and Aylesbury, now arrived at Rickmansworth. By September 12, 1960 steam workings would be pushed further out as the electrification went forward to Amersham.

R M Casserley

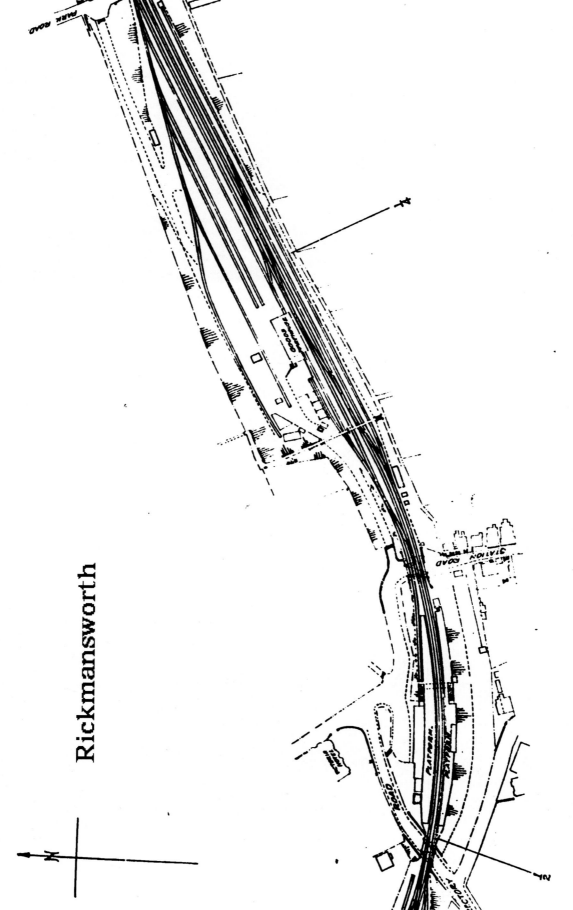

Rickmansworth

Rickmansworth station in 1908

John Mock Collection

With absorption of GCR Joint arrangements on the line by the LNER in 1923 shared working continued on, effectively with Chiltern Railways to the present day. Here an heroic image of the LNER is caught on camera at Rickmansworth with V2 2-6-2 60863 on a Marylebone to Manchester train on July 23, 1955.

H C Casserley

Electrics abound, with a fine view of the goods shed and coal facilities at Rickmansworth. So substantial a structure makes the point that the Met sought a greater role than just a suburban passenger carrying railway.

John H Meredith

Engines of the Met's own 'K' class were sold off to the LNER after November 1, 1937 to continue in their natural environs for a few more years until their withdrawal in the late 1940's. Two were scrapped in 1943, one 1945, one in 1946 and two in 1948 This photograph is evocative, but less creditworthy of the care taken by the LNER of former Met engines that normally appeared in a presentable, if not always highly polished state. In fairness it should be pointed out that both no 6160 with the 'up' local train and L48 on stand-by duty appear to have suffered the vagaries of the recent war that afflicted all railways, this view on April 27, 1946.

H C Casserley

The closing years of their working lives, one of the MetroVick locos no 3 'Sir Ralph Verney' at Rickmansworth in August 1961.

D M Hibbert

The year of 1947 deserves this sunny day of July 26, having endured one of the worst winters of the century. Here a peaceful scene in the bay at Rickmansworth as L48 simmers patiently in the role as standby engine for main line failures. With such an intensive service the line had to have precautions like this

R M Casserley.

Waiting steam in the leafy Chilterns, as the steam locomotives wait, one to carry trains foward from the electrics on the larger tank engine an L1 67781 of the Eastern Region. And the smaller ex Met standby engine both seen here on June 3, 1956 . Quite often the Met locos were used to haul the through City - Chesham trains, especially on Saturdays.

R M Casserley

The mix of steam and electric with a train arriving from Baker Street behind no 10 'William Ewart Gladstone' that is now simply 'W E Gladstone'. Engine 42249 has just detatched from an 'up' and will then reverse to the 'down' line and pass through the station to the stableing sidings north of the station, 'down' side; July 23, 1955.

H C Casserley

Early Metropolitan, June 4, 1904, with three panel livery on 0-4-4 former 'E' class no 77 with condensing pipes for working underground. Note Met crest on front splasher.

R K Blencowe

British Railways tank engines of the Standard class operated some of the Met services with 80144 on the regular Aylesbury to Liverpool Street service on August 29, 1959. Here it was detached and replaced with an electric loco .

H C Casserley

An evocative year for the Met, April 22, 1933, in this view of no 5 'John Hampden', arriving in Rickmansworth with a 'down' Baker Street to Aylesbury train waiting to detach.

H C Casserley

Quintessential Metro-Land maturing in 1955 near Harrow, London side. Images of summer, bright sunshine, with a train passing the lines of confidant villas, domestic harmony between city and countryside complete.

RAS Marketing

The new Uxbridge Metropolitan Railway station on Belmont Road prior to electrification.

Hillingdon Heritage Service

Chapter Five
The UXBRIDGE BRANCH

The Uxbridge branch was opened on Thursday June 30, 1904, a seven and a half mile branch from Harrow; named 'The Harrow & Uxbridge Railway' (Act August 6, 1897) to join originally with the Ealing and South Harrow line of the District Railway. Their plan to extend a line to Beaconsfield and High Wycombe was opposed by the GWR who were successfully entrenched with their Wycombe Railway at the latter town.

A further Harrow & Uxbridge Act of August 9, 1899 authorised a branch of 1 mile 12 chains between Rayners Lane and Harrow, this was cancelled with the District and the option was taken up by the Metropolitan, still reserving running powers to the District. The H&U subscribed £1,200 towards the building of the line. So keen was the town to break the GWR monopoly for passenger trains and goods traffic.

Finally, on a fine summer day, with a heavy scent of new mown hay prevailing, much of it bound for London stables; most of the line was enclosed by woods and fields. The first Uxbridge train clattered by garlanded with flowers, the name of the town prominent on the front of the engine. As blooms fade, so did the image of such a scene, as electricity soon replaced steam on the line

At Uxbridge a large marquee 100ft long by 40ft wide enclosed a sumptious feast as the Chairman Colonel J J Mellor regailed them all with his delight at the prospects of the new line to the town. The station building was in red brick and neatly laid out on land that had formerley been for recreation, for circuses and shows,

situated at the corner of the York and Belmont Roads. The platform was 540 feet in length.

The line, in its short length required 28 bridges and at the South Harrow end a viaduct of half a mile long with no less than 71 arches. At Harrow a bay platform was provided for a shuttle service in addition to through workings.

From the outset the line was being prepared for electricity with a sub station being built at Ickenham. Only one station existed en route at the opening, this was at Ruislip.

Construction began in September 1902 when 600 men set to work under the instruction of one Mr E P Seaton, MICE engineer of the line with contractors messrs Bott & Stennett.

The Met introduced its first multiple unit electric services on January 1, 1905 between Baker Street and Uxbridge. The branch had in fact only seen steam locomotives for six months.

Electric track between Rayners lane and South Harrow was introduced on March 1, 1910. Thus the special train on the opening day with invited guests of the Chairman and board of the Harrow & Uxbridge Railway joined with the Metropolitan Railway who would work the line.

Fares on day of opening from Uxbridge to Baker Street 2 shillings (10p) 1st class; 1s 3d (6p) 2nd; 1s 1d (5p) 3rd. Return 3s (15p); 1s 10d (9p); 1s 6d (7½p). Workmen's tickets 7d (2½p).

From Uxbridge to Ruislip single 6d (2½p), 4d (2p), 3d (1½); return 9d (3½), 6d (2½), 5d (2d). Season tickets Uxbridge to Aldgate for twelve months £21. One month £2 2s. Second class £17 and third £1 14s, third class £14 and £1 8s.

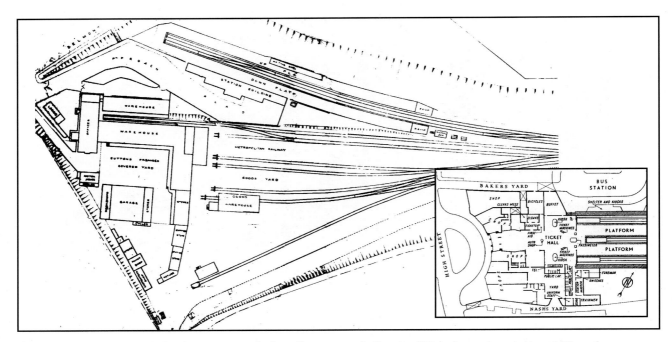

The original station at Uxbridge, very much the all accommodating traditional country station. Although electricity soon took over the passenger work, steam would continue with the goods trains. A new resited station would see the changing profile of the Met with higher density passenger requirements. Inset new station layout.
Mike Crosbie Collection

The townspeople of Uxbridge may have regarded the branch as being overdue in terms of the needed competition with the GWR but it was right on the mark for electrification. Improvements did not remain there, although what developed next had to wait until after the first world war.

With the investment of the new works programme of London Transport many stations received improvements, following on from the hitherto piecemeal and varied standards of former company stations. Uxbridge station was not very old as stations go, just over thirty years, but it was decided to replace and resite it. The new station was to be on the High Street, extended from York Road.

The remarkable feature of the new station was its design. The concept of the old station was decidedly nineteenth century country station style. The new station was definitely twentieth century, the architect Charles Holden created the ultra modern suburban look, seen also in the rebuilding of Harrow and Rayners Lane. The entire station level was lowered to bring it to street level. It could not have a simpler design for access of large volume passenger movement. The rails now entered along a cutting of concrete retaining walls with the platforms enclosed inside prefabricated concrete sections supporting a glazed roof. The ticket windows neat and accessible but arranged to one side of the main hall to keep as

much clearance as possible. There was also a modern refreshment room.

The interior retains this strong period flavour to the present day. The crescent shaped front presenting the new dynamic impression that LT were so keen to create with the modern thinking of architects and artists. Over the slightly art deco entrance are sculptures of two

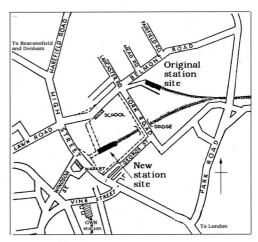

Re-siting of the station terminus at Uxbridge from the Belmont Road site to the High Street. Obviously this would require the building of the York Road bridge Note the Vine Street station of the GWR that could not withstand the introduction of the improved Met facilities. It closed to passengers on September 10, 1962, for freight on July 13, 1964. Uxbridge High Street (GWR) closed to passengers August 31, 1939 and to goods September 25 1939 with coal trains lasting to 1962.

Electrics, early Ashbury with later tube stock.alongside. The occasion was the opening of the Piccadilly Line service on October 23, 1933. East Barnet was the original name of Cockfosters. The new service created greater demand on the line with new housing being built alongside.

Hillingdon Libraries

speeding wheels collecting electric power reinforcing the concept.

A significant advantage to the branch was that population increased rapidly along its length. This created demand for intermediate stations Ickenham Halt opened September 25, 1905. Ruislip Manor Halt August 5, 1912. also Eascote that was handling as many as 1½

million passengers per year and was rebuilt in 1937.

District line trains ran into Uxbridge from 1910. They were joined by the Piccadilly line trains that ran to South Harrow and on to Uxbridge on October 23, 1933. District line trains are believed to have ceased during World War 1.

Timetable for the Baker Street to Uxbridge services in 1909.

Bill Simpson Collection

Uxbridge station which had been the more commonplace country branch line terminus when it opened. With the expansion of the town much more was needed for the new commuters in the thirties, resulting in this spectacular design of the period by Charles Holden. A clear wide pathway at street level and entirely covered. Light concrete, roof glazing and tiled surfaces give the interior a light airy feel and the rich county crest glass panels add a splendid dash of colour. The different ages and designs of Ruislip, Hillingdon and Uxbridge provide a variety of interesting historic comparisons in station architecture. These photographs taken in 2002.

Bill Simpson

The only negative feature is that trains arrive and depart in a concrete cutting as this electric locomotive on July 4, 1954

R M Casserley

The front of the station has this superbly balanced crescent, now paved, which was once intensly used by traffic including trolley buses.

Bill Simpson

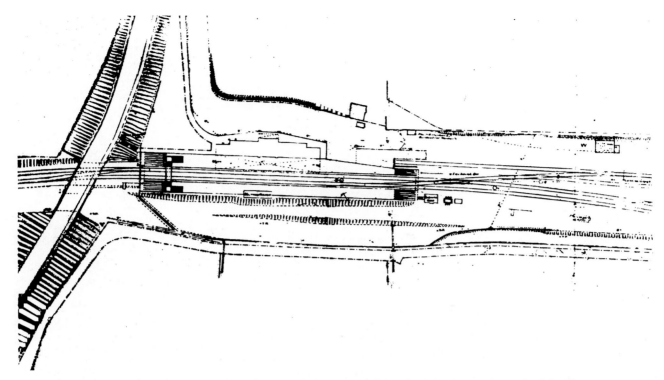

Ruislip station in 1905 note the original entrance from the 'up' side alongside the road overbridge. The station building pattern was virtually the same as Uxbridge and remains to this day as an original station on the line. One time goods facilities were on the Harrow side of the station.

Mike Crosbie Collection

Front elevation and plan view of Ruislip station with its facilities noted below.

Mike Crosbie Collection

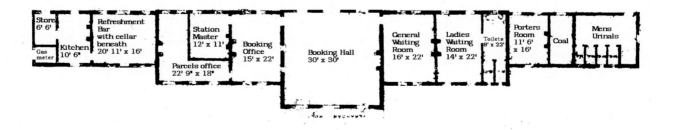

Ruislip station which remains in the pattern adopted for the Metropolitan branch, an unremarkable but robust design. Removal of decorative valancing and barge boarding, probably during re-roofing, has reduced much of the attraction of its original appearance. This photograph taken as below in 2002.

Bill Simpson

More interesting is the platforms side with this delightful lattice footbridge. The pantiled roof was a later addition. The lever frame signal box cabin represents one of a diminishing quantity of such structures, once the most common of all on railways.

Bill Simpson

Elevated West Harrow station with the booking office on the opposite side of the bridge. This view on January 18, 1933
London's Transport Museum

The original Hillingdon station of the Metropolitan Railway now totally rebuilt in glowing white and glass due to the road alterations nearby.

London Underground Railway Society

Presenting the final days of the Metropolitan, Stanmore station buildings of 1932 repeat Clark's rus-in-urb style used at Watford, here with attractive hipped roof dormer windows. This upper floor being rented as accommodation. Stanmore of course became part of the new Bakerloo Line, now Jubilee and represented the final statement of Metropolitan Railway expansion and development. The photograph is during the early London Transport days.

London's Transport Museum

Chapter Six

The STANMORE BRANCH

The name Wembley, that had once been the name for a small country village, acquired an association that passed into the national conciousness, everyone came to know the meaning of the name with its sporting connotations. To be called to attend some great sporting moment was focal point of many sporting people's lives, to say that it would be at Wembley meant to enter the grand arena where legends are created.

The beginning of Wembley's own recognition must be circumscribed into the history of the Metropolitan Railway who opened a station there on October 14, 1893 on their extension from London into what would be enchantingly promoted as 'Metro-Land'.

Now that great stadium is no more, after standing for some time with its vast and silent space still filled with the ghostly sense of the accumulative roar of triumph from so many

years' events. Events like the British Empire Exhibition of 1924-25, the exhibition buildings themselves now remain forlornly as goods warehouses. But the exhibition stimulated further the interest in industry, homes and civic amenities in the district. So successful was Wembley to the Metropolitan that the railway decided to seek powers to extend from there to Stanmore, deeper into the greensward of rural Middlesex. Construction of this new line would also include the quadrupling of the main line between Wembley and Harrow and re-signalling. This was entrusted under the Developments Loans Guarantees & Grants Act of 1929. The Met had been interested in a branch from Wembley to Stanmore, Bushey and Watford, negating the need for two separate branches. Whatever, in the first decade the Met were not disposed to follow up such a scheme and the war reduced such enterprises.

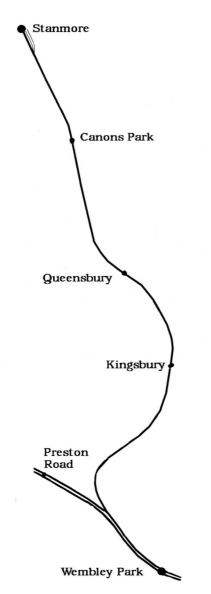

The four mile branch to Stanmore, prospectively planned with possible extension to Elstree.

Stanmore was not entirely virgin railway territory as the LNWR had a 2 mile 8 chain branch from Harrow & Wealdstone. Neverthless the Met considered Stanmore as a prospect in their role of a developer to rural parts of the line,

They began construction of their branch in 1929 from a point between Wembley Park and Preston Road, taking a 15 chain radius curve. When completed it would be four miles from the main line junction, which itself is seven miles from Baker Street. At the outset this would be a completely electrified line, with power sub stations at the junction and another near Canons Park Edgware. Power was supplied from Neasden at a pressure of 11,000 volts that were stepped down with static transformers and converted into direct current at 600 volts by rotary converters, three installed at Preston

Road and two at Canons Park Edgware. Automatic colour-light signals were installed to control the traffic between the junction and the terminus, the points and signals being remotely operated from Wembley Park signal cabin.

The line opened on Friday 9, December 1932 with the first train consisting of two 1930 motor coaches, three first class trailers with a Pullman car and the Metropolitan directors saloon. Conveyed to the opening were Mr Pybus the Minister of Transport with the Chairman of the company Lord Aberconway and other officers of the company. All of which was, in true style of the Met, forever publicity conscious, with a significant press entourage. Mr Pybus performed the opening ceremony and the line was down to the serious business of working London commuters the following day. The branch had three original stations of Kingsbury, Canons Park and Stanmore which had an island platform. Another station called Queensbury between Kingsbury and Canons Park was opened by the LPTB on December 16, 1934.

Signalling came under the control of Wembley Park signalbox with a subsidiary signalbox at Stanmore. The lines were served by 144 trains daily with the fastest trains reaching Baker Street in twenty-two minutes; with through trains operating in busy periods, whilst a shuttle operated to Wembley Park in the quieter hours.

To operate this and other branches the Met introduced sixty-five new coaches for multiple unit working that were built by the Birmingham Railway Carriage & Wagon Co and were called MW stock, but later with LT became 'T' stock, the last being withdrawn by LT in October 1962.

The Stanmore branch and its new stock was to be the swan song of the Metropolitan Railway, for on July 1, 1933 the lines of this and other companies became part of the unified body of the London Passenger Transport Board.

The LPTB wasted little time in making their mark with the New Works Programme (£45,000,000) in 1935. The Metropolitan line had faced an intensity of use and the Stanmore branch could only increase that density of traffic. It was decided therefore to construct a $2\frac{1}{2}$ mile line of tube railway off the Bakerloo Line to run between Baker Street and Finchley Road. This was a reapprasial of an earlier Met plan of 1925 for deep level tube between Edgware Road and Willesden Green to solve the same problem.

To speed up the service Bakerloo Line trains would run alongside the former Met stations calling at intermediate stations as far as Wembley Park. Consequently the Stanmore branch became part of the tube system still

First day train on the branch.

capable of taking standard loading guage stock. The line of the miniscule St John's Wood railway that began the original extension now ceded from the Met by new stations on the tube line.

The plans included reconstruction of Finchley Road station with a cross platform interchange. The old order of the running lines from left to right had been - Down Local; Up Local; Down Fast; Up Fast. The new order became Down Fast; Down Local; Up Local; Up Fast. Other stations were rebuilt which brought the new '30's look'. At Wembley Park the Stanmore line was diverted into a burrowing junction. The Bakerloo extension was opened on December 20, 1939, previously the burrowing junction had been used by Metropolitan Line trains.

The branch retains its Metropolitan line flavour in its stations with short canopies. Queensbury, which was an addition by London Transport has seen a great deal of development since 1934.

The Bakerloo Line ran with six car trains so in order to facilitate seven car trains platforms were lengthened from 291 ft to 377ft with required modifications to the tube tunnel.

Other alterations included moving the old island platforms at Dollis Hill and West Hampstead from between the 'up' and 'down' locals which became respectivley 'down fast' and 'down local' . The new arrangement accommodating the Bakerloo Tube. Also involved in the conversion was Kilburn into an island platform with the old 'down' platform being abolished.

The changes were carried out on the weekend of November 5/6 1938 between Preston Road to Dollis Hill including the burrowing junction to Stanmore from Wembley Park. On the weekend of September 18, 1939 the work was completed from Dollis Hill to Finchley Road. At Wembley Park a new 'up' bay platform was provided to deal with special traffic concerning Wembley Stadium.

All the booking halls at West Hampstead, Kilburn, and Dollis Hill were completely modernised.

An important advantage to the new track layout was from the time of the opening of the Stanmore branch the fast and local lines exchanged places causing trains to cross each others path. The new diagram removed this risk situation. Burrowing Junctions had now been provided for the Stanmore Branch and the access for Neasden car depot.

In 1971 construction began of the Jubilee Line which took over the Stanmore Branch of the Bakerloo Line. Now that the LNWR/LMS line is a distant memory the line continues vigorously serving the suburb of Stanmore.

Days in steam on the Stanmore branch, tank engine L44 hauling electric stock at Stanmore on October 1, 1961
H C Casserley

Additional sidings were installed at Stanmore for storing the stock to operate the Bakerloo service. This view in summer 2002.
Bill Simpson

The 'up' Aylesbury Pullman hauled by Metropolitan Railway no 3 British Westinghouse locomotive in 1910.
Ian Allen Ltd

Black Five no 44895 near Northwood with the with a 'down' 2.38 ex-Marylebone to Nottingham on April 30, 1966.
K C H Fairey

Electric locomotive no 8 'Sherlock Holmes' at the unrebuilt Moor Park and Sandy Lodge on August 29, 1959 with a train for Liverpool Street.

R M Casserley

Bradshaw's timetable for the through workings of branches of the former Metropolitan in 1942. This includes the Stanmore branch, which at this time was on the Bakerloo line
Bill Simpson Collection

Watford station on August 4, 1954 with one of the T stock electric units.

Alan Jackson / London Underground Society

Chapter Seven

The WATFORD BRANCH

Watford was one of the original stations of the London & Birmingham railway main line. that in 1846 passed into the combine of the London & North Western Railway. The LNWR was therefore well established when the Metropolitan decided that it would annexe some of the traffic from this developing town of some 30,000 people. A highly industrialised town of brewing, paper and printing, it was a prize worth the attention of the Met.

When the L&B drew up their survey in the early 1830's a problem at Watford was a large tract of land north of the town at that time called the Cassiobury Estate which was on land owned by the Earl of Essex who was very much opposed to allowing the railway access over his land. The consequent diversion ensured that the L&B would have to dig an expensive mile long tunnel and divert the railway away from the central point of the town, being accessed by a long road, requiring an omnibus service. The LNWR did consider extending their Stanmore branch to Watford, making Wembley the Junction in 1892, but this was not a popular idea.

However the Watford Tradesmen's Association must have found a single company serving the town to be uncompetitive and made their own approach to the Metropolitan in 1895, suggesting a branch via Stanmore from Wembley Park. The Met had arrived at Rickmansworth in 1887 only just over two miles away to the west. At the time they were involved very much in their northern extension with the lines to and beyond Aylesbury to build and consolidate.

Not to be denied, for they must have been very dissatisfied with the railway monopoly of the town, the Tradesmen tried again in 1903. This time they had the support of the Urban District Council. The Met were now busy with the electrification of the Uxbridge branch and must have felt capitalised to the hilt, apart from a direct clash with Euston. Neverthless the Watford lobby had enough strength of determination to prevail and arranged to meet the Met in February 1904 when they were again deferred. Watford interests strenghened their arm still further by acquiring a petition of 1,402 signatures for a branch from the Met at Rickmansworth. A problem for the Met was that their Joint partner the GCR had not recovered from the immense expenditure of their London extension.

111

The Met decided to survey a possible route in October 1906. A problem was the same contentious piece of land Cassiobury Park which had resolutely stood against the London & Birmingham.

The route chosen for a survey was south-east of the Watford - Rickmansworth Road along the valley of the River Gade. Predictably in 1907 the LNWR decided to promote a spur from its Rickmansworth branch (1862) of just over a mile to Croxley Green. The Met petitioned that this branch should be constructed in such a way that it does not impede any route surveyed by the Met.

On this basis the LNWR were successful with their Act on July 26, 1907. The Met pensively viewed the progress of the LNWR who had already begun a motor bus service from Watford Junction station to Croxley Green on April 23, 1906. The LNWR branch was laid to Croxley Green as far as Cassio Bridge, in fact the terminus was a mile from the centre of Croxley. On this branch a West Watford station was opened on the very edge of town facing the sewage farm. Operating a shuttle a service of trains from June 15, 1912. An extension of the bus service continued on into Croxley Green.

Shortly after the LNWR had proceeded events concerning Cassiobury Park took an upward course for the Met. Some of the land of the estate came onto the market and was purchased by a building syndicate with 50 acres to Watford Urban District Council. A station site was agreed and the Metropoiltan re-surveyed their route, further north than the first. A Bill was deposited for the session of 1912 seeking powers for the Metropolitan & GCR Railways to construct a branch from Croxley Hall east of Rickmansworth station to Watford, a few yards west of the Hemel Hempsted Road, just over two miles. After passing through the east end of Croxley Green the line ran along the north-west of the main road, skirted the north-west edge of Watford, north of the Grammar School and crossed Cassiobury Park on an embankment varying in height from six to eleven feet before entering a 17ft 6in deep cutting in which the terminus was to be situated. The junction with the main line was to have two spurs towards Rickmansworth and towards London. An intermediate station was proposed at Croxley Green and there was to be a Halt to serve Watford Golf Course. The route was difficult insomuch as it was at odds with the landscape cutting across the Chiltern rift of the Chess and Gade Rivers and involving a crossing of the Gade Valley before entering Watford.

The support of Watford Council proved somewhat conditional and they could not support a line across the newly released Cassiobury Park. This forced the Met to cut it back to the proposed goods yard near the Grammar School, far remote from the desired position in the centre of the town.

As the Met pursued its option the LNWR and the Underground Company were negotiationg the possibility of running tube trains over the LNWR to Watford. Apart from the LNWR there was one other objection from a landowner, this latter type of objection was often to increase the compensation. The LNWR rather loftily considered 47 'up' and 49 'down' trains to Euston and 7 trains each way to Broad Street sufficient to the needs of 2,700 passengers. Obviously the impending competition was foreseen as a threat to the LNWR, discarding any advantage to rail users. The LNWR was a main line company and could not increase trains to the extent of the Met and GCR Joint which had specifically planned to be a suburban commuter railway. To compete the LNWR made much of their plans from the Act of 1907 for suburban electric trains and work had started in 1909. These plans included a tube tunnel under Euston but together with the Underground Company another, better scheme evolved. This was to extend the Bakerloo tube from Paddington to Queens Park and thence to Watford. The Bakerloo had been extended from its original line of 1906 from Elephant and Castle to Baker Street to Edgware Road in 1907. Now under the London Electric Bill of 1912 it received the Royal Assent to continue to Paddington 1913, Queens Park 1915 and finally Watford in 1917. The LNWR were so keen to see this line built that they loaned to the Underground Company £1 million at 4 per cent to build the Paddington - Queens Park section. They claimed that Watford would have the advantage of three routes into London, to Euston, to Broad Street and the Bakerloo, with all stations to the Elephant & Castle. The LNWR's attitude was virtually dismissive of the Metropolitan plans which probably incensed them as being treated as minor upstart company, when in fact they had become a powerful force in London. The Metropolitan was also dismissive of the LNWR's Croxley Green branch as a poor unremarkable effort. Whatever, the Met & GCR Joint Act was passed in August 7, 1912 to form the Watford Joint Railway Committee. The LNWR had managed to force on the Met a raising of their embankment over the Gade Valley to allow for an underline bridge, should it be required by the LNWR, who claimed that they would one day extend their branch to Tring, a mere punitive ploy.

The Met proceeded with negotiations for land and the LNWR proceeded with their electric line but the first World War happened on August 4, 1914 which held plans in reserve, greater issues came to the fore.

Finally electric traction reached Watford on the Bakerloo and LNWR trains began on April 16, 1917, taking just over an hour for the twenty miles or so to London. The LNWR to Broad Street via Primrose Hill

The LNWR line began to run their own electrics to Euston and Broad Street on July 10, 1922. The Croxley Green branch was electrified in October of the same year with a shuttle service to Watford Junction and through trains at peak times to Rickmansworth Church Street.

Still none of this distracted the Met & GCR Joint, they could see the potential at Watford and they continued with their plans aided by the passing of a Trade Facilities Act in 1921 which offered Treasury guarantees on capital to promote employment. Consequently construction began in 1922 on a contract placed with Logan & Hemingway of Doncaster. The Line was difficult as much of it was elevated above the Gade Valley. Passing over a number of public roads, the Grand Union Canal and the River Gade from a very high elevation. The eventual station was situtated on the area designated for the goods yard as the Met & GCR Joint had been frustrated from entering the town to a High Street site which was very much what they wanted. From this frustration an arcane little story developed of a Watford Development Company that purchased a property roughly in line with the new branch on the other side of Cassiobury Park. This was called Derby House which on purchase they proceeded to demolish and replace with a structure intended for a restaurant and winter gardens but had an uncanny resemblance to the style of the Metropolitan station buildings. The building front assiduously carried timetables and advertising information for the Met & GCR, when it was opened on July 15, 1916. Further, a strip of land that was part of the same lot, at the back of the building continued the alignment of a potential railway. Whatever could be deduced from this, the property remained in various commercial uses. It was sold by the LPTB in 1950 and is now a pub/restaurant.

Securely Cassiobury Park has remained unsullied as a local amenity and Watford Metropolitan station characteristically continues in business surrounded by mature leafy villas frustratingly far from the High Street but certainly the pleasanter by location.

Construction of the line bridged the grouping of 1922-23 and consequently the line was opened by the joint companies of the Metropolitan and the London & North Eastern

Railway, who had absorbed the interests of the former Great Central Railway. The line was managed by a Watford Joint Railway Committee.

The double junction north and south affords train access to the locations of the LNER and the south to the new modernised London complex. The new line of two miles and a half cost about £300,000. As a result of the Metropolitan main line between Harrow and Rickmansworth being electrified from January 5, 1925 the Watford line was electrified from the outset. Also operated with the latest automatic signalling.

Watford platform length of 615ft and 30ft wide, with a 280ft wood and glass canopy supported on steel girders. Entrance to the station is from Cassiobury Park Avenue with an additional piece of 40ft roadway.

Work on the line was Supervised by Mr E A Wilson Chief Engineer of the Metropolitan Railway for both companies. The resident Engineer being Mr J Martin Clark. The station buildings were designed by Mr C W Clark Architect of the Metropolitan Railway. Contractors were Messrs Logan and Hemingway of Doncaster and steelwork for the bridges was supplied by Messrs Eastwood, Swingler Co of Litchurch, near Derby.

The train service began on Monday 3rd November with 40 trains each way daily mostly by the Met to Baker Street and from there to Euston Square, Kings Cross, Farringdon and High Holborn, Moorgate and Liverpool Street. The LNER ran a service to Marylebone both termini being reached in about half an hour. A service to Rickmansworth began on the same day.

A capacious goods yard and goods shed was provided for the movement of goods and livestock with cattle pens and horse dock. This had seven sidings and a five ton crane.

The Rickmansworth north curve was utilised much for goods traffic but passenger traffic was vulnerable to bus competition and regular passenger trains ceased in January 1934. Sunday services in use to January 3, 1960 with the occasional early morning train running to this day.

On October 2, 1925 an inspection by Lt Col A H L Mount on behalf of the Board of Trade was undertaken, He recommended trap points to protect the junction lines from runaway on the 1 in 100 climb to Croxley.

On the Saturday, before the opening to the public, a train left Baker Street at 11.50 am and called at Croxley Green at 12.18, then arrived at Watford at 12.20. Five minutes later the train that left Rickmansworth at 12.20 called at Croxley Green at 12.23 then ran into Watford

WATFORD'S NEW RAILWAY

METROPOLITAN AND L.N.E.R. JOINT EFFORT

THE new double-track Extension line, jointly constructed by the Metropolitan and London & North Eastern Companies, to Croxley Green and Watford, is now an accomplished fact and will be opened for traffic on Monday next, 2nd November.

New Route to the Midlands, and the North, etc.

A northerly Junction will permit of a Service being maintained from Watford to Rickmansworth, Chesham and Aylesbury, and various stations north of this point, both on the Metropolitan and L.N.E.R. systems, and will also provide Watford with a direct means of access to numerous important districts in the Midlands, the North of England and Scotland.

New Line's Many Advantages.

The new line offers many advantages. It will make Watford—Hertfordshire's largest and most important town—easier of access; open up an unique residential district offering unlimited scope for building operations, and, at the same time, materially improve Watford's transport facilities. The new Watford station is conveniently situated on the South-west side of the town at a point where housing development is especially active and immediately adjoins, in particular, the extensive Cassiobury Park Estate.

Cost £300,000 to Construct.

The new line, although only 2¼ miles in length, has presented considerable difficulty in construction, and has cost no less than £300,000 to complete. It has been equipped for electric traction, and protected throughout its entire length by the latest type of automatic signalling, and everything conducive to the comfort and convenience of the travelling public has been carried out.

140 Trains Daily.

The train service provided over the new route is particularly liberal, totalling no fewer than 140 trains daily. A proportion of these will be operated electrically by the Metro. to Baker Street and thence through to City stations, whilst the London & North Eastern Railway will introduce a new service of steam operated trains to and from Marylebone. The journey time from Watford to Baker Street and Marylebone, respectively, is approximately half-an-hour. Quarterly, Monthly, and Seven-Day Season Tickets are issued; special fares for workmen provided and also Cheap fare and Excursion facilities afforded.

Map:
TO RICKMANSWORTH CHESHAM, AYLESBURY ETC, ETC   WATFORD
CROXLEY GREEN
MOOR PARK & SANDY LODGE
NORTHWOOD
PINNER
NORTH HARROW
HARROW ON THE HILL
TO MARYLEBONE
TO BAKER ST. CITY AND WEST END STATIONS.

Goods Traffic Facilities.

The Joint Companies have arranged to deal with all classes of Inwards and Outwards Goods, Mineral and Live Stock traffic. Motor vehicles will be utilised for both collection and delivery of traffic received from or despatched to any station on the Metro., L.N.E.R., G.W.R., Southern Railway, etc. To efficiently handle this traffic, extensive sidings, adequate cart roads, stacking grounds, cattle pens, and horse and carriage dock, have been provided and arrangements made for dealing with Parcels, Perishable and other traffic, to all parts of the United Kingdom by passenger train.

Help to Local Industry.

The new railway will provide a direct link with towns, coalfields and districts in the Midlands, the North of England, and Scotland, and will materially assist local industry by placing it in communication with a wide range of manufacturing and other districts, from which to secure, to greater advantage than in the past, such essentials as coal, building materials, steel work, manufactured articles.

Prior Opening of Stations.

The new Croxley Green and Watford Stations will be open on and from Wednesday, 28th October, 1925, for the purpose of giving particulars of Season Ticket Rates, Train Services, etc. Quarterly, Monthly and Seven Day Season Tickets can be obtained in advance at these Stations. Further information on any subject affecting the new line will be gladly given on application by the Commercial Manager, Metropolitan Railway, Baker Street Station, London, N.W.1, or the Passenger Manager, London and North Eastern Railway, Liverpool Street Station, London, E.C.2.

TRAVEL BY THE NEW ROUTE – EASIEST AND BEST

The new railway goes all out with new publicity to draw passengers away from the existing LMS line

Watford Observer

alongside the earlier train on the opposite platform.

An assemblage headed by Lord Aberconway, Chairman of the Met and Lord Farringdon deputy Chairman of the LNER with many VIP's including Sir Harry Verney and Mr R H Selbie General Manager of the Met alighted from the train and were met by the Mayor of Watford Alderman R A Thorpe and members of the council.

A luncheon took place at the Oddfellows Hall where the leaders of the two railways spoke glowingly of the railway and the town having reached a kind of 'marriage' along a rocky path. Plans might have been brought to a conclusion in 1912 but for the intervention of the war. However the companies were confident that their contribution to Watford with its burgeoning industry will be a fruitful one for both. The Mayor and corporation thanked the railwaymen and spoke of having provided a direct pathway across Cassiobury Park and a large residential development was now being developed around the station. Consequently the Council felt vindicated by refusing to allow the railway to cross the park as they had hoped as the ground will now have rail users living close by. The Metropolitan directors must have smiled wistfully at this purported advantage. Two railways had been thwarted by the Park from reaching the High Street where they would be in a better position to compete with the Junction and the LMS High Street station.

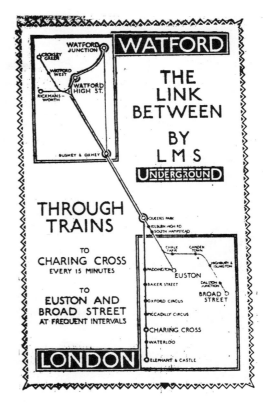

The LMS vigorously reply to the opening of the Met line with their own publicity.

Watford Observer

The Mayor spoke of a new line also coming from Edgware. This is the proposed Northern Line that was never built, the Bakerloo, later Jubilee being the actual alternative.

Watford in the early sixties

London Underground Society

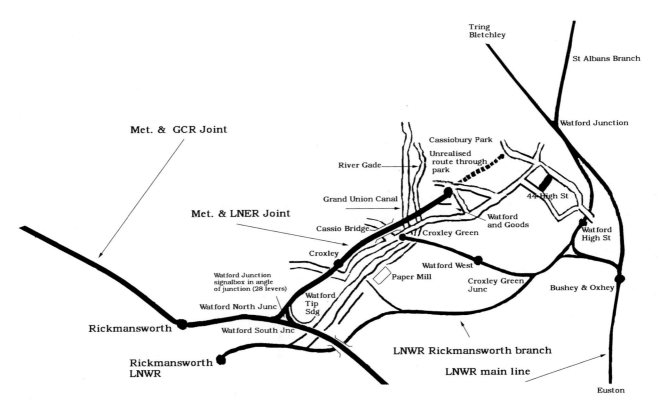

The new Met line at Watford compared to the former LNWR competing lines. Note the LNWR line to Watford West and Croxley that the LNWR claimed that they may one day wish to extend to Tring.

Number 44 High Street, Watford, the Met's hoped for railway station providing convenient access in the very centre of the town. Problems emanating from the obstruction of Cassiobury Park were never resolved and it remained in various other uses. It is now one of the Wetherspoon chain of pub/restaurants under the romantic name of 'Moon Under the Water'.

London Underground Society

Croxley Green, just over a mile from the junction, the only station between the Junction and Watford on the slightly over two mile branch. It was named simply 'Croxley' to avoid confusion with the other station on the former LNWR branch. This view on March 10, 1968.

John Edgington.

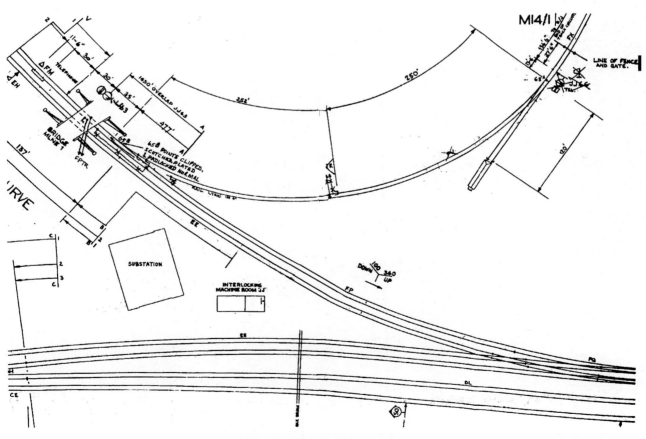

Watford tip siding at the junction.

Mike Crosbie Collection

Croxley station buildings an attractive assembly in brick and tile with the upper floor enclosed in gables, this photograph in 2002.

Bill Simpson

The 20 lever signal box at Croxley in all timber, often done to save excess weight. The signalbox became redundant for use during the reorganising of the four-track installations on the main line in the 1960's. Thenceforth the signalling was operated from Rickmansworth. For a time it remained in use to operate the goods yard until that function also became unnecessary. It has now been demolished, this view on March 10, 1968.

John Edgington

Terminus building at Watford shortly after opening in 1925. More remote from the centre of the town than the Met would have liked though attractively enclosed facing nearby Cassiobury Park.

Mike Crosbie Collection

Construction on the site of Croxley green station in the early twenties.

Mike Crosbie Collection

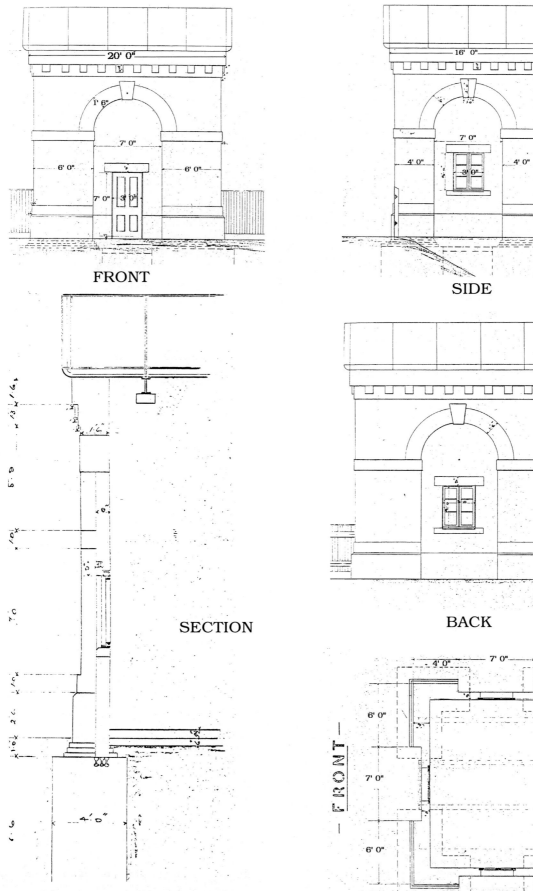

FRONT

SIDE

SECTION

BACK

The water tank house on the platform at Rickmansworth

Mike Crosbie Collection

PLAN

LOCOMOTIVES

When the Metropolitan Railway became part of London Passenger Transport Board on July 1, 1933, it was the only constituent company to bring steam into the group. The number of steam locomotives of the Met had to increase to cope with the railway's expansion northwards.

In 1933 the remaining part of the system that was still worked by steam was from Rickmansworth to Verney Junction. Including the branch lines from Chalfont to Chesham and from Quainton Road to Brill. All goods trains were steam hauled.

The steam locomotives were split into seven types and classified with letters A, C, D E, F, G,

H, K, all of them being tank engines. Two locos unclassified by letters were two 0-6-0 saddle tanks used for shunting in the goods yards at Neasden and Harrow These were Nos 101 and 102 built by Peckett & Co in 1897.

At first Met engines had been painted in dark green but at about the time of completion of the Circle it changed to the characteristic deep rich red. At first the engines carried their numbers raised in brass on the front of the chimney, when the new livery was adopted it was painted on the tank sides. All locos were left hand drive.

Ex GWR pannier tank, the Metropolitan began with GWR steam and ended with GWR steam, under the aegis of London Transport. Engine L90 was one of the 0-6-0 tanks that was formerly numbered 7760. It was one of the locomotives built by the North British Loco Co in 1930, seen here at Neasden in October 1958 remaining beyond its peers until 1971.

R M Casserley

The short wheelbase saddletank locos became the engine type that epitomised the requirement of the thousands of marshalling yards and industrial sidings throughout Britain. They existed in their thousands, ingloriously labouring amongst the acres of wagons and vans. At all hours of the clock they pulsed their exhaust, hissed and clanked back and forth, the only sounds in a slumbering town or city. This smart little engine was one of two that performed such duties for the Metropolitan at Neasden.

both H C Casserley

Bunker first view of 101. Having so few steam locomotives compared with the larger companies they were able to revere even this humble workhorse with full livery, even lining on the wheels! Many private engines fulfilling the same kind of role were painted in varied colours, scarlets, strident light blues and bright toy like greens. Practically speaking it did give them high visibility in the darkness of sheds, yards and factories.

R K Blencowe

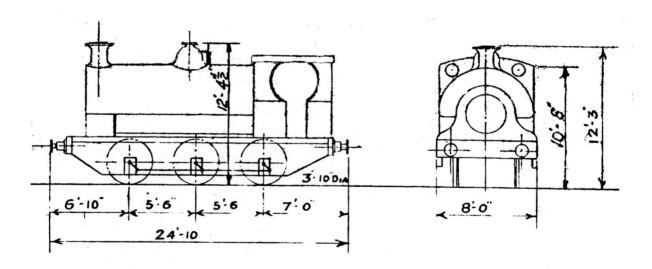

Class 8										
No	Type	Date	Mkr	Name	Boiler	cyls	Length	dw/bogie	weight	scrap/sold/comment
101	0-6-0ST	1897	Peckett & Co		140 lbs per sq in	16 x 22		3ft 10 ins	39	LPTB no L53, withdrawn 1960
102	-	1899								LPTB no L54, withdrawn 1961

A class 'A' engine in its early form with three panel lining and the oval logo enclosing the number. Obviously, the early engines, in keeping with other railways, were without cab roof and sides, seen later as below. Note the considerable space between the bogie wheels and the driving wheels to allow the engines optumum flexibility on tight curved track. Had they not been so built it would have been impossible for them to have been used on the Brill Tramway, a line whereupon they became super power. See below, modified without condensing pipes and a magnificent gleaming brass ßdome, engineman's pride!

London Underground Railway Society Collection

Under the gathering clouds of war in the sultry summer at Lillie Bridge on July 14, 1939, a London Transport 'A' class L45. A hardy survivor that was formerly Met no 23, habitue of the Brill Tramway. Now back in London it eventually found preservation and now resides in the London Transport Museum at Covent Garden.

H C Casserley

A Class

The 'A' class 4-4-0T once totalled 66 all built by Beyer Peacock & Co between 1866 and 1885. The 66 were at one time divided into A and B classes. The 'B' class numbered 34-38 and 50-66 but most had all gone by 1933. This left five 'A' class, these were nos 23, 27, 41, 48 and 49, they were used mainly on permanent way trains and shunting at Neasden. They also operated the Brill branch. These engines were only 12ft 5in high and 31ft 5in long, obviously an advantage for the narrow confines of some parts of the system. Engines after 1870 were fitted with the Adams sliding bogie in place of a Bissel truck, a design that had been used on a former LBSCR loco. The first 18 locos were delivered by BP in 1864 (works nos 412-429), no 23 was one of a batch of five, nos 19-23, that were built in 1866, (works nos 706-710). The building dates, railway numbers and works numbers of the remainder were as follows 1868 nos 24-28, (770-774), and nos 29-33, (853-857). In 1869 no 39, (868), nos 40-43, (893-896), nos 45-49, (863-867); 1870-no 44, (897).

Similar engines were built for the North London Railway in 1865, the Midland in 1868 and the London & South Western in 1875 while some also went abroad to the Rhenish Railway in 1871. One of the Met engines was sold to the Mersey Railway. They were all fitted with condensing pipes. but it is doubtful if these locomotives could have worked efficiently for prolonged periods under those conditions with constant condensing. Full advantage was taken of the fact that they could run as non-condensing in the open. The condensing equipment being brought into operation in tunnels. The period of condensing was hampered by comparatively low water capacity as the tanks held only a 1000 gallons. These became hot themselves which was not desirable as it affected the injectors. Some early locos were fitted with pipes across the boilers to carry away steam. The water towers and tanks at Aldgate, Edgware Road and Kensington High Street, must have been frequently used to replenish water.

Class A

No	Type	Date	Mkr	Name	Boiler	cyls	Length	dw/bogie	weight	scrap/sold
1	4-4-0	1864	BP	Jupiter	120 lbs sq in later 160 lbs	17¼ x 24 ins	33ft 1 in	5ft 10 in 2ft 117/8	45 tons (42.2?)	1897
2	-	-	-	Mars	-	-	-	-	-	Withdrawn 1907
3	-	-	-	Juno	-	-	-	-	-	Withdrawn 1907
4	-	-	-	Mercury	-	-	-	-	-	Withdrawn 1906
5	-	-	-	Apollo	-	-	-	-	-	Withdrawn 1906
6	-	-	-	Medusa	-	-	-	-	-	Withdrawn 1906
7	-	-	-	Orion	-	-	-	-	-	To Mersey Railway in 1925 as '2'
8	-	-	-	Pluto	-	-	-	-	-	Withdrawn 1907
9	-	-	-	Minerva	-	-	-	-	-	Withdrawn 1906
10	-	-	-	Cerebrus	-	-	-	-		To Cambrian Rly as '2'
11	-	-	-	Latona	-	-	-	-		To Cambrian Rly as '12'
12	-	-	-	Cyclops	-	-	-	-		To Cambrian Rly as '33'
13	-	-	-	Daphne	-	-	-	-		To Cambrian Rly as '34'
14	-	-	-	Dido	-	-	-	-		To South Hetton Coal as '36'
15	-	-	-	Aurora	-	-	-	-		To Cambrian Rly as '36'
16	-	-	-	Achilles	-	-	-	-	-	Withdrawn 1907
17	-	-	-	Ixion	-	-	-	-	-	Withdrawn 1907
18	-	-	-	Hercules	-	-	-	-	-	Withdrawn 1926
19	-	1866	-		-	-	-	-	-	Withdrawn 1911
20	-	-	-		-	-	-	-	-	To Nidd Valley Lt Rly
21	-	-	-		-	-	-	-	-	Withdrawn 1906
22	-	-	-		-	-	-	-	-	Withdrawn 1925
23	-	-	-		-	-	-	-	-	Became LT no 45
24	-	1868	-		-	-	-	-	-	Withdrawn 1913
25	-	-	-		-	-	-	-	-	Withdrawn 1913
26	-	-	-		-	-	-	-	-	Withdrawn 1925
27	-	-	-		-	-	-	-	-	Withdrawn 1935
28	-	-	-		-	-	-	-	-	Withdrawn 1906
29	-	1869	-		-	-	-	-	-	Scrapped 1925-
30	-	-	-		-	-	-	-	-	Withdrawn 1907
31	-	-	-		-	-	-	-	-	Withdrawn 1906
32	-	-	-		-	-	-	-	-	Withdrawn 1906
33	-	-	-		-	-	-	-	-	Withdrawn 1906
34*	-0-6-0	1868	-Worcs		-	-	-	-	-	To Taff Vale Rly
35*	0-6-0-	-	-Engine	Built by Worcester Engine Co and designed by R H Burnett, later became Superintendent for the Metropolitan, for the St Johns Wood Railway. It was a powerful design to lift trains out of Baker Street over the gradient to cross the Regents Canal. They were sold off and their role was supplanted by 4-4-0's.				-	-	To Taff vale Rly
36*	0-6-0-	-	-Co					-		To Sirhowy Rly
37*	0-6-0-	-	-						-	To Taff Vale Rly1907
38*	-0-6-0	-	-					-	-	To Taff Vale Rly
39	-	1869	-					-	-	Withdrawn 1906

Class A

No	Type	Date	Mkr	Name	Boiler	cyls	Length	dw/bogie	weight	scrap/sold
40	4-4-0	1870	BP		130 ibs sq in later 160 lbs	171/4 x 24 ins	33ft 1 in	5ft 10 in 2ft 117/8	45 tons	Withdrawn 1906
41	-	-	-		-	-	-	-	-	Scrapped 1936
42	-	-	-		-	-	-	-	-	Withdrawn 1925
43	-	-	-		-	-	-	-	-	Withdrawn 1913
44	-	-	-		-	-	-	-	-	Withdrawn 1925
45	-	-	-		-	-	-	-	-	Withdrawn 1906
46	-	-	-		-	-	-	-	-	Withdrawn 1927
47	-	-	-		-	-	-	-	-	Withdrawn 1906
48	-	-	-		-	-	-	-	-	Withdrawn 1936
49	-	-	-		-	-	-	-	-	Withdrawn 1936
50*	-	1879	-	-	-	-	-	-	-	Withdrawn 1907
51*	-	-	-		-	-	-	-	-	Withdrawn 1911
52*	-	-	-		-	-	-	-	-	Withdrawn 1907
53*	-	-	-		-	-	-	-	-	Withdrawn 1907
54*	-	-	-		-	-	-	-	-	Withdrawn 1906
55*	-	-	-		-	-	-	-	-	Withdrawn 1906
56*	-	-	-		-	-	-	-	-	Withdrawn 1907
57*	-	-	-		-	-	-	These three locos were originally delivered to the South Eastern Rly in 1880. The Metropolitan took possession of them in 1883	-	Withdrawn 1907
58*	-	-	-		-	-	-		-	Withdrawn 1911
59*	-	-	-		-	-	-		-	Withdrawn 1911
60*	-	-	-		-	-	-		-	Withdrawn 1907
61*	-	-	-		-	-	-	-	-	Withdrawn 1907
62*	-	-	-		-	-	-	-	-	Withdrawn 1907
63*	-	-	-		-	-	-	-	-	Withdrawn 1907
64*	-	-	-		-	-	-	-	-	Withdrawn 1907
65*	-	-	-		-	-	-	-	-	Withdrawn 1911
66*	-	1885	-		-	-	-	-	-	Withdrawn 1906

* Engines originally that formed the B Class used for working the District lines and became modified class 'A' s. Engine no 1 was involved in an accident at Baker Street in September 1897 and was subsequently scrapped.

The survivor of the class, no 23, ran with the Met from the time it was delivered until 1905 when the line was electrified to Harrow. From then until 1914 it headed trains between Baker Street (from Harrow), Rickmansworth, Chesham and Verney Junction, So many years in the gloom it now ran in the open country. After which it was relegated to shunting at Neasden and occasional freight and coal train working. From goods and shunting it went back to passenger work on the Brill branch from Quainton Road, until 1935. It was finally withdrawn in 1948, when it worked engineers trains and shunted at Neasden and Lillie Bridge. A highlight of the loco's career was in 1934 when, on one occasion, it was pressed into service to bring an 'up' eleven coach LNER express from Leicester into Marylebone, the train locomotive had failed at Aylesbury. It made its journey to preservation on January 15, 1961, from the Neasden depot of LT to the British Transport Museum at Clapham. Its final number was L45 in LT's fleet. It was restored externally to its 1903 condition. It had been rebuilt three times in its life, in 1889, 1903 and 1918. It is now in the LT museum at Covent Garden.

No 48 at Neasden, an engine that also saw service on the Brill Tramway. Interestingly this design of engine, specified for its flexible wheelbase, was done to accommodate the Tudela & Bilbao Railway. In the situation of one of those occasions of fortunate coincidence, it was just what the Met was looking for. This one is seen here at Neasden on July 11, 1936.

Authors Collection

In original beautifully kept condition one of the District Railway Beyer Peacock 4-4-0's no 38. Note the pipe over the boiler to release water vapour heated in the tanks.

H K Blencowe

A 'C' class engine no 70 in the livery style at the turn of the century with single panel on tank sides, later it would be simplified further with 'Metropolitan' in sans serif lettering.

C Class

This locomotive class was probably some influence of Sir Edward Watkin as they had a strong similarity to the South Eastern Railway types. They were delivered in June 1891 and fitted with condensing pipes, but not regarded to have done much condensing, as they worked in the open sections of the northern extension. With the intense development of the line through the heavily graded Chilterns something greater than the lighter 'A' class tanks was needed. Some rebuilding was done to them in 1901-3, but they were eventually replaced by the even more robust 'H' class. They were the first locomotives to carry totally enclosed cabs.

No	Type	Date	Mkr	Name	Boiler	cyls	Length	dw/bogie	weight	scrap/sold/comment
67	0-4-4T	1891	Neilson& Co Designed by		140 lbs per sq in	17 x 26	-	5ft 6ins	50.4 tons	Withdrawn 1917
68	-	-	J Stirling		-	-	-	-	-	Withdrawn 1923
69	-	-	-		-	-	-	-	-	Withdrawn 1923
70	-	-	-		-	-	-	-	-	Withdrawn 1923

A "Sharpie" 'D' class in workshop grey from which can be deduced that this is prior to its introduction in 1895. Although intended for the lines north of Aylesbury the latter four were fitted with condensing pipes.They were fitted with Cortazzi type axleboxes which allowed one inch side play.

R M Casserley Collection

Class D

Built for goods trains and to work the Aylesbury - Verney Junction and Brill lines, on the latter in particular they proved too heavy. They replaced the borrowed LNWR engines that had run the Aylesbury & Buckingham service until April 2, 1894. The new 'D' class took over that service on February 1, 1895. Like the 'C' class they were eventually replaced by the 'H' class locomotives. Engines 71, 73, 74, 75, 76 were sold to the Ministry of Munitions. Engine 72 was sold to Charles Williams, Morriston, South Wales.

No	Type	Date	Mkr	Name	Boiler	cyls	Length	dw/bogie	weight	Withdrawn/scrap
71	2-4-0T	1894	Sharp Stewart		150 lbs per sq in	17 x 26	-	5ft 3ins	43.5	Withdrawn 1920
72	-	-	-		-	-	-	-	-	Withdrawn 1916
73	-	1895	-		-	-	-	-	-	Withdrawn 1920
74	-	-	-		-	-	-	-	-	Withdrawn 1921
75	-	-	-		-	-	-	-	-	Withdrawn 1921
76	-	-	-		-	-	-	-	-	Withdrawn 1921

At Neasden 'E' class loco now preserved at the Buckinghamshire Railway Centre.

R K Blencowe

Class E

The 'E' class 0-4-4T's were built to replace the 'A' class on the main line. They were a design created by T F Clark Chief Mechanical Engineer of the Metropolitan. In 1933 all seven were still in use They had a water capacity of 1250 gallons.

They worked all the main line trains until the 'G' class in 1915 but were not seriously displaced until 1920 when the 'H' class appeared. Even at the very end in 1933, one could still be seen working the Chesham branch. Fortunately one of the class was purchased by what was then the London Railway Preservation Society,

now (Quainton Railway Society) at the Buckinghamshire Railway Centre on March 20, 1964. There it was restored to steam in 1986, the only former Met engine that can now claim that distinction. It can occasionally be seen in steam at the centre near Quainton Road station beautifully restored in its Metropolitan livery. Part of its remarkable past was the fact that it ran the first passenger train up the Uxbridge branch. Happily it was as able to repeat this duty on the anniversary of the line in July 1960. Not many engines could claim first and last!

No	Type	Date	Mkr	Name	Boiler	cyls	Length	dw/bogie	weight	scrap/sold/comment
1	0-4-4T	1896	Built by Metropolitan Railway at Neasden		150 lbs per sq in	17 x 26	-	5ft 6in	54.5	Originally allocated class A Into LPTB ownership LPTB No L44 Withdrawn 1963
					-	-	-	-	-	-
77	-	1896	-		-	-	-	-	-	Went into LPTB ownership as no L46
78	-	1896	-		-	-	-	-	-	Went into LPTB ownership Withdrawn 1935
79	-	1900	Built by Hawthorn, Leslie							Still in existence at end of metropolitan Withdrawn 1935
					-	-	-	-	-	
80	-	1900	-		-	-	-	-	-	Went into LPTB as no L47; scrapped in 1941
81	-	1901	-		-	-	-	-	-	Became LPTB no L48 Withdrawn 1963/Scrp '64
82		1901								In existence at end of Metropolitan Withdrawn for sale 1933

Another view of an 'E' class at Neasden of L48 on October 4, 1958 smartly presented in London Transport livery

R M Casserley

Like a parade of Metropolitan steam the far 0-6-0 saddletank, the 'A' class no 48 and leading is an 'E'; class no 82. Note the combination of couplings on the buffer beam.

R K Blencowe

Class 'F' at Neasden on July 11, 1936

H C Casserley

Class F 0-6-2T

The 'F' class 0-6-2T's had only four in the class. Except for an extra pair of coupled wheels they were very like 'E' class. The four were built in 1901 by the Yorkshire Engine Co. to take up on the work too heavy for the 'E' class.

Their intended use was for freight and coal trains. Weight 56 tons cyls 17¼ x 26 in working pressure 160lb. Coupled wheels 5ft; heating surface 1,150 sq ft. After 1933 they were used on light goods train and for shunting purposes, and a great deal on the quadrupled section of the main line from Wembley Park and Harrow. Also used in the construction of the new Stanmore branch with support of the 'A' class engines.

No	Type	Date	Mkr	Name	Boiler	cyls	Length	dw/bogie	weight	withdrawn/scrap
90	0-6-2	1901	Yorks Eng							Became LPTB no L49 Withdrawn 1957
91										Became LPTB no L50 Withdrawn 1958
92										Became LPTB no L51 Withdrawn 1957
93										Became LPTB no L52 Withdrawn 1962 Sc 64

On sidings at the power station at Neasden 'F' class no 92.

R K Blencowe

An 'F' class in the LT number of L49 originally Met no 90. This view at Neasden June 22, 1946.
Brunel University Transport Collection

The altogether bulkier appearance of the Jones engines brought in the latter period of the Metropolitan, with engines that look very representational of a main line company. Electrification was now the power of the Circle and City lines but out in the Chiltern reaches came these handsome designs.

R K Blencowe

Class G 0-6-2T

The 'G' class consisted of four 0-6-4T mixed traffic engines, they were the only named locomotives remaining in Met stock. Nos 94-97 named: 94 Lord Aberconway, 95 Robert H Selbie, 96 Charles Jones, 97 Brill.

They were built in 1915 by the Yorkshire Engine Co and had two inside cylinders 20in x 26 in; working pressure 160lb; 5ft 9 in coupled wheels. Total heating surface 1,361 sq ft, weight 73 tons. Boilers much larger than older engines and with Belpaire fireboxes, piston valves and Robinson superheaters. They had Wakefield mechanical lubricators and the first to have piston valves. Another design by Charles Jones. They were all sold to the LNER on November 1, 1937.

No	Type	Date	Mkr	Name	Boiler	cyls	Length	dw/bogie	weight	scrap/sold/comment
94	0-6-4T	1915	Yorks	Lord Aberconwy	160 lbs per sq in	20 x 26		5ft 9ins	73 tons	To LNER in Eng. Co 1937 as M2
										6154 Withdrawn 1946
95	-	1916-		Robert H Selbie						LNER 6155 Withdrn 1948
96	-	1916		Charles Jones						LNER 6156 Withdrn 1948
97	-	1916		Brill						LNER 6157 Withdrn 1943

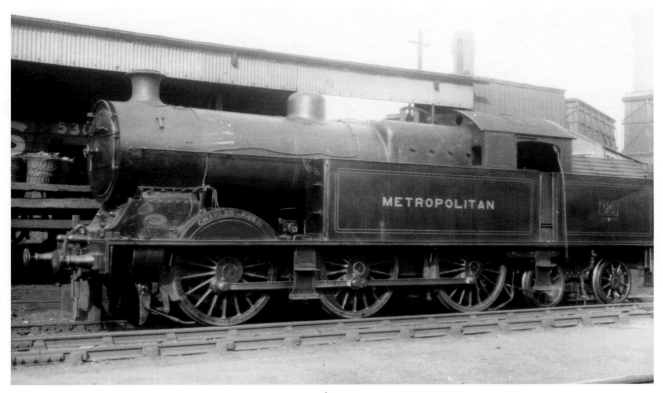

One of the 'G' class engines no 96 'Charles Jones'.

R K Blencowe

Engine no 97 simply called 'Brill', the remote village in Buckinghamshire that had a terminus station on the Metropolitan Railway.

R K Blencowe

Engine no 105 at Neasden on January 1, 1934

R K Blencowe

Class H 4-4-4T

The eight 'H' class 4-4-4T's (superheated) were popularly received engines and made the final statement for the standard passenger locos on the railway. After an interval of 23 years design went back to outside cylinders and a leading bogie. They were the work of Mr Charles Jones Chief Electrical & Locomotive Engineer and were all built in 1920 by Kerr, Stuart & Co. They numbered 103-110 and became the main passenger engines on the line until the end. Their excellent acceleration between regular stops, together with flexible wheel base, allowed them to negotiate sharp curves on the branches with through trains, which made them ideal. They were needed also for the heavier rolling stock on trains to Aylesbury.

Later they were equipped with Belpair fireboxes and Walshaert's valve gear, the first Met engines to be so fitted.

Nos 106, 108, 109 and 110 were fitted with plain smokebox doors of the Maunsell SECR pattern, while 106, 109 and 110 had their uncased Ramsbottom safety valves replaced by Ross Pop valves. When the LNER assumed responsibilty for passenger services north of Rickmansworth in 1937 these locos became nos 6415 to 6422. They were transferred to the former GCR shed at Neasden from where, for several years, they continued to work passenger trains north of Rickmansworth. All were however withdrawn from service by 1947. Engine no 108 was fitted with Scarab system of oil burning in 1921. At the same time two boilers at Neasden power station were also converted.

Class H										
No	Type	Date	Mkr	Name	Boiler	cyls	Length	dw/bogie	weight	scrap/sold/comment
103	4-4-4T	1920-21	Kerr Stuart		160 lbs per sq in	19 x 26		5ft 9ibn	77 tons	To LNER in November1937 class H26415 Withdrn 1946
104	-	-								LNER 6416 Withdrn 1947
105	-	-								LNER 6417 Withdrn 1947
106	-	-								LNER 6418 Withdrn 1946
107	-	-								LNER6419 Withdrn 1943
108	-	-								LNER6420 Withdrn 1946
109	-	-								LNER6421 Withdrn 1942
110	-	-								LNER6422 Withdrn1946

Engine 105 seen with the Neasden loco coal road just behind.

Bill Simpson Collection

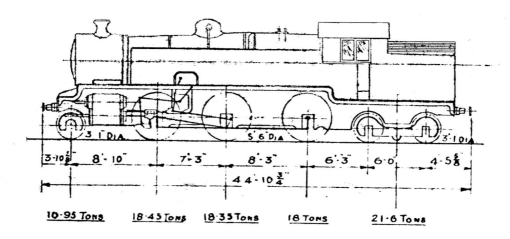

A 'K' class 2-6-4T

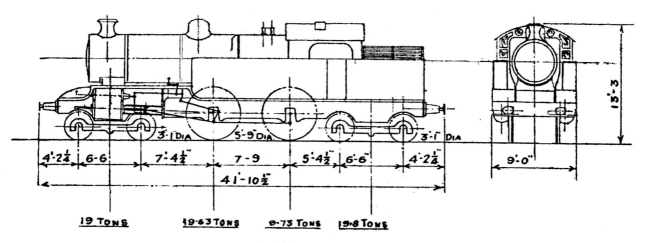

An 'H' class Jones 4-4-4T

Large handsome engines, much bigger than anything that the Met had previously used and a fitting final statement on the railway's steam power. This view of 115 at Neasden c1937

R K Blencowe

K Class 2-6-4T

The Met built only six of these impressive engines nos 111 to 116, they did haul passenger trains but their prime intention was the goods traffic north of Harrow or Finchley Road.

Before 1925 most of this was handled by 'A', 'F' and 'G' classes. In 1925 these larger powerful 2-6-4T engines were purchased from the government. They had been constructed at Armstrong Whitworth with parts from Woolwich Arsenal, just after the war, to the designs of Mr R E L Maunsell, then of the SECR. They had all the characteristics of the 2-6-0 tender engines common on the Southern Railway. Except for smaller driving wheels they were generally similar to his SECR '790' class 2-6-4T which became the Southern Railway 'River' class tank engines, having the coned boiler and back sloping Belpair firebox crowned with Ross Pop valves. They had two outside cyls 19in x 28in, working pressure 200lbs 5ft 6in coupled wheels, heating surface 1,811 sq ft, weight 87 tons 7 cwt, superheated. They were confined to lines north of Finchley Road where they were used on heavy freight trains. They were out of gauge for the tunnel sections.

Class K										
No	Type	Date	Mkr	Name	Boiler	cyls	Length	dw/bogie	weight	scrap/sold/comment
111	2-6-4T	1925	Armstrong Whitworth /Woolwich Arsenal		200 ilbs per sq in	19 x 28		5 ft 6 in	87.35 tons	Designed by R Maunsell Transferred to LNER November 1937 Became class L2 6158 withdrawn 10/48
112	-	-								6159withdrawn1/43
113	-	-								6160 wirhdrawn 10/48
114	-	-								6161 withdrawn 5/43
115	-	-								6162 withdrawn 1/46
116	-	-								6163 withdrawn 5/45

This three quarter view presents 116 outside the steam shed at Neasden on July 11, 1936, by now painted with London Transport on the sides. The cab could be totally enclosed as the side windows could be slid across.

H C Casserley

Final ownership was with the LNER with whom they entered stock under their numbering scheme, thus engine 116 became 6163. This view is at Stratford on a sunny August 8, 1935.

H C Casserley

Far from the environs of Baker Street was the Wotton Tramway that by absorption came into Met ownership under the grandly modified ambitions of the Oxford & Aylesbury Tramway. Part of the modifications was the introduction of three Manning Wardle saddletanks. The first name of this engine was 'Earl Temple' after the builder of the Wotton Tramway. Later it was changed to 'Brill no 1'. In this view the train has stopped at Westcott one of the stations along the six mile line. The driver leaning on the cab side is the irascible Harry Cross, the young lady, Miss Mary Varney was the porter and crossing keeper. This line will be studied in detail in book three of this series.

Buckinghamshire Railway Society

Saddletanks

Class ST Shunter

No	Type	Date	Mkr	Name	Boiler	cyls	Length	dw/bogie	weight	Withdrawn/Scrap
100	0-4-0ST	1886	HC						22 tons	Withdrawn 1907

Class 0-6-0ST

No	Type	Date	Mkr	Name	Boiler	cyls	Length	dw/bogie	weight	Withdrawn/Scrap
	0-6-0ST -	1876 1894	MW -	Wotton No 1 Brill No 1 Wotton No 2					18 tons	Withdrawn 1901r Withdrawn 1915 Withdrawn 1915

Wotton no 1 was originally named ' Huddersfield' the engine was purchased by the Oxford & Aylesbury Tramway in 1894. It was eventually sold to Phillips of Newport Monmouthshire in 1901.
Brill no 1 was originally named 'Earl Temple'. It was sold to T W Ward Ltd, Sheffield. Then to Frank Hayes of London.
Wotton No 2 was bought by the O&AT in 1899. Then sold to T W Ward, Sheffield. Later sold to Holland, Hannen & Cubitts.

Class ST Shunter

No	Type	Date	Mkr	Name	Boiler	cyls	Length	dw/bogie	weight	Withdrawn/Scrap
	0-4-0ST	1867	MW	NELLIE					16 tons	Shunter

Hired (bought) from Eckersley & Bayliss who had used it during the construction of the Uxbridge branch. From 1907 to 1915 it was used for doing shunting work at Neasden.

One of the 'A' class locomotives in early cabless form with the Hammersmith destination board. Judging by the position of the water bag on the side where the driver is looking, the engine is probably in process of replenishing its supplies suggesting possibly that this is Hammersmith.

R K Blencowe

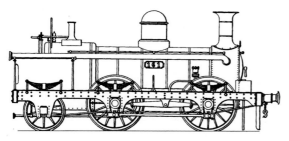

First locomotive loaned to the Metropolitan Railway by the Great Northern Railway in the emergency of 1863 when the quarrel with the GWR led to them removing trains. It was built by Tayleur & Co and sold to the GNR in 1850.

1

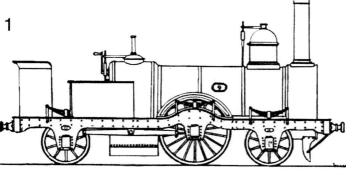

Other locomotives were improvised nos 1 and 2 were tender engines that had their frames lenghened to the rear of the driving wheels by 3ft 1in increasing their wheelbase from 12ft 8 in to 15ft 9 in. This was to accommodate a large water tank and and a coal bunker so that they could work as tank engines. Fig 1, engine number 9 had a certain degree of end play to the trailing axles to allow lateral movement on sharp curves. New engines, Fig 2, engine number 241,were built to work GNR trains on the underground by Avonside Engineering in 1865. These had four coupled wheels in front and a single pair of trailing wheels with radial axleboxes under a large coal bunker. Condensing was provided by a long pipe running below the footplate into the tank.

Dimensions were; cw 5ft 6in; tw 4ft; cyls 61/2inches by 22ins. Boiler barrel length 10ft by diameter of 4ft. Firebox casing 4ft 6 ins total heating surface 867.7 sq ft. Total weight in working order 39 tons 12 cwt 2qtr

2

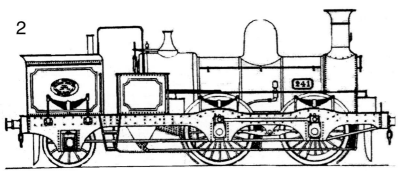

The new electric locomotives of 1904 with British Westinghouse equipment, the 'Camelbacks' were the first design of electric loco for the Metropolitan and followed in the principle of a Central London Railway design. Not an unqualified success, as the position of the cab and and controls suggested a back to back steam locomotive with the motorman always looking over a protrusion. Much more successful were the following ten with British Thomson Houston equipment with the motorman positioned right for the new concept, immediately at the front with maximum visibilty.

Metro-Cammel loco 1904 steeple cab

No	Type	date	Mkr	bought	wheelbase	HP	Name	dw	scrap/sold/comment
1	Bo-Bo	1904	Metro-Cammell	1904	24ft 9in	800		3ft 2in	Westinghouse Eqipment
2	-	-	-	-	-		-	-	-
3	-	-	-	-	-		-	-	-
4	-	-	-	-	-		-	-	-
5	-	-	-	-	-		-	-	-
6	-	-	-	-	-		-	-	-
7	-	-	-	-	-		-	-	-
8	-	-	-	-	-		-	-	-
9	-	-	-	-	-		-	-	-
10	-	-	-	-	-		-	-	-

Built by Metro-Cammel with the BTH equipment loco no 20 a conclusion had not yet been reached, but the design concept was clear. The outline of the subsequent Vickers to follow can be easily discerned.

London Underground Society

British Thomson Houston

No	Type	date	Mkr	bought	wheelbase	HP	Name	dw	scrap/sold/comment
11	Bo-Bo	1906	Metro-Cammell	1906	24ft 6in	800		3ft 2in	BTH Equipment
12	-	-	-	-	-	-	-	-	-
13	-	-	-	-	-	-	-	-	-
14	-	-	-	-	-	-	-	-	-
15	-	-	-	-	-	-	-	-	-
16	-	-	-	-	-	-	-	-	-
17	-	-	-	-	-	-	-	-	-
18	-	-	-	-	-	-	-	-	-
19	-	-	-	-	-	-	-	-	-
20	-	-	-	-	-	-	-	-	-

In 1922, twenty of these Metro-Vick locos became the staple traction loco for Met electric traction for trains first to Wembley Park, Harrow then Rickmansworth, only leaving London Transport in 1961/2 The patriotic names they carried were an excellent publicity boost. A marked contrast to the electrification of British Railways in the sixties onwards, when some names had the reverse effect by being trivial. This view of no 1 'John Lyon' taken in 1933.

H C Casserley

Metro-Vick Loco

These locomotives were supplied to the Met by the builders Metropolitan-Vickers Electrical Co Ltd of Trafford Park, Manchester. The haulage requirement stipulated for them was on trains of six standard bogie coaches weighing, with passengers, about 180 tons; addition of the locomotive brought the weight to 240 tons. They were employed on the service between Aldgate and Bishop's Road on a duration of nineteen minutes each way. To do this the designer estimated that the locomotive would be required to have maximum power requirement of 60 watts per ton per mile. In practice this proved well sufficient as the actual requirement was 55 watts per ton per mile. The wheel arrangement of 0-4-4-0 (two bogies) carrying a

body with a 300 hp self ventilated motors driving the running axles through single reduction gears, total hp being 1,200. As the numbers of the class increased they displaced their forbears and were employed on the Met to Harrow and then to Rickmansworth.

Prior to 1961 nos 9, 15, 17, 19,and 20, were withdrawn. The remainder of the class followed in September 1961. Four; no 1, 'John Lyon', no 3, 'Sir Ralph Verney', no 5, 'John Hampden' and no 12 'Sarah Siddons' were retained for shunting purposes and adhesion tests which included 2, 7, 16, 18. They were finally broken up by Thos W Ward Limited of Sheffield. With the exception of no 12 which remains in the London Transport Museum at Covent Garden.

No	Type	date	Mkr	bought	wheelbase	HP	Name	dw	scrap/sold/comment
1	Bo-Bo	1922	Metro-Vickers	1922	29ft 6in	1,400	John Lyon	3ft 2in	Metro-Vick Equipment
2	-	-	-	-	-	-	Oliver Cromwell	-	later Thomas Lord
3	-	-	-	-	-	-	Sir Ralph Verney		
4	-	-	-	-	-	-	Lord Byron		
5	-	-	-	-	-	-	John Hampden	-	
6	-	-	-	-	-	-	William Penn	-	
7	-	-	-	-	-	-	Edmund Burke	-	
8	-	-	-	-	-	-	Sherlock Holmes	-	
9	-	-	-	-	-	-	John Milton		-
10	-	-	-	-	-	-	William Ewart Gladstone	-	
11	-	-	-	-	-	-	George Romney	-	
12	-	-	-	-	-	-	Sarah Siddons	-	
13	-	-	-	-	-	-	Dick Whittington	-	
14	-	-	-	-	-	-	Benjamin Disraeli		
15*	-	-	-	-	-	-	Wembley 1924		
16	-	-	-	-	-	-	Oliver Goldsmith		
17	-	-	-	-	-	-	Florence Nightingale		
18	-	-	-	-	-	-	Michael Faraday		
19	-	-	-	-	-	-	John Wycliffe		
20	-	-	-	-	-	-	Sir Christopher Wren		

The first locomotive in traffic bearing nameplates was no 17 'Florence Nightingale' on October 3, 1927.
Number 15 'Wembley 1924' was shown at the British Empire Exhibition as 'BEE 1924'.
No 10 was originally proposed 'Sir Francis Drake' whilst no 16 deferred 'Charles Dickens' and 'Anthony Trollope' for 'Oliver Goldsmith' The names finally adopted of were done because they represented people that had in some way been associated with the Metropolitan Railway.
*The nameplate of number 15 was surmounted by the British Lion. In 1943 removal of the bronze nameplates was a wartime measure though not all were removed. One plate was to be preserved in the LPTB museum. Locos due for painting were painted grey due to scarcity of paint and easier to keep clean.

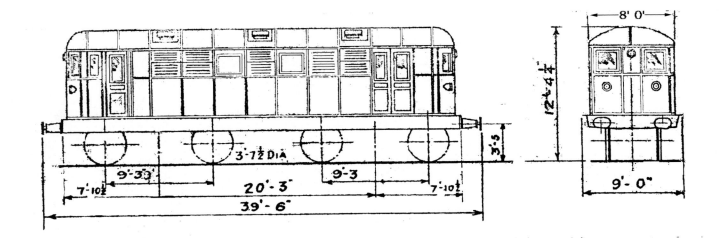

Apparently ready for the days duties at Neasden in March 1933. Engine no 14 'Benjamin Disraeli' with Liverpool Street headboard and behind no 9 'John Milton' with Aldgate headboard.

H C Casserley

The Metropolitan, rightly, took appearances very seriously, the typography and beautiful small ornamental flourishes at each end of the nameplate represent the artistic style of art nouveau in a very evocative way.
This noticeably contrasts with the art deco world that followed with Gill Sans for London Transport.

H C Casserley

Electric units

Brown Marshalls were absorbed by the Metropolitan Amalgamated Railway Carriage & Wagon Co that produced the first electrics for the Metropolitan Railway in 1905. These units were the first electrics on the Uxbridge branch. Each car over 52 ft long and 8 ft 9ins wide with transverse as well as longitudinal seats, with sliding doors and swing gates, as a result of serious draught problems the gates were replaced with doors. Also with electric lights and heating. Motors are carried two motors per bogie on each train under second class cars, four motors on each car of 150 hp each giving every motor car 600 hp each bringing the driving power of each train to 1500hp. They had the latest electro pneumatic train control. There are no power cables through the train as each car collects its own power Further cars differed with manufacturers being Westinghouse and British Thomson Houston. They were finished in varnished teak with mouldings in pale yellow and waist and cant rails painted in cream. Similar stock of BTH equipment was run on the Hammersmith & City Joint as 'Great Western & Metropolitan Railway' cars.

London Underground Society

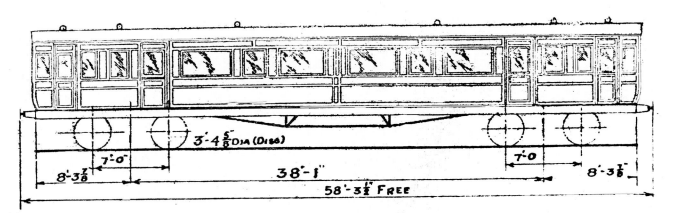

The Rothschild saloon, which was in effect two 32ft vehicles spliced together. It was originally intended for use of the baron and his staff, very much competing with the LNWR for VIP usage. Later it was used by the board of directors of the Metropolitan Railway. It was also made available for Lt Col A H L Mount on his inspection of the Watford branch. Most remarkable of all was that it was used by the LT board to go on a final inspection of the rickety Brill branch, what a splendid sight it must have made in the tiny Brill station.

Mike Crosbie Collection

One of the '1921' stock motor cars no 117. These were intended for speedier loading at stations with double sets of sliding doors. They were tried successfully on the Inner Circle and consequently appeared on services of the developing Uxbridge branch.

London Underground Society

Coach no 486 on a train at Harrow April 20, 1958.

R M Casserley

Circle line train entering Moorgate in early 1950's. Note canopy support on right divested of its purpose by wartime bombing.
London Underground Railway Society

A District 'G' class motor car at rear of this eastbound train at Moorgate on August 3, 1962.
P W Boulding / London Underground Railway Society

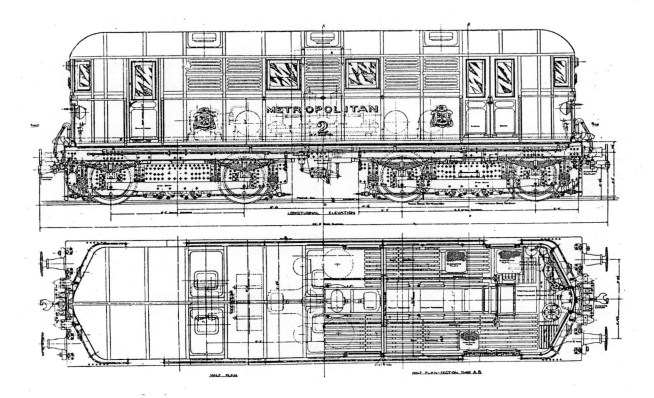

ELECTRIFICATION

Electrification was going to be a necessity by the turn of the century, the Central London Railway had proved its worth, if any was needed, for the enormous capital expenditure that would be necessary. The Met was no longer unchallenged in its prime mover role, local omnibuses proliferated and affected returns. Indeed the Met itself had contributed to this competition by operating its own trams and buses.

At the outset power was the main problem, with trains of some 160 tons sharply accelerating on severe gradients with regular stops. An exhibition at Crystal Palace in 1882 had demonstrated drawing electric power from a third rail.

Both the Met and the District experimented with third rail direct current system. The Met had done their own experiments at Wembley Park earlier. The Joint experiment was on the Earls Court to High Street (Kensington) section of line. This was fed by a small temporary power station at Earls Court for 600 volts dc. The undertaking was directed by Sir John Wolfe and Sir William Preece. Another experiment was conducted between Notting Hill and Praed Street from May 21, 1900 to November 6, 1900 with motor coaches that had four gearless motors situated on each axle. It was completely successful and ensured that full installation was to be undertaken straight away.

The six coach train was fitted with Siemens motors, with three coaches each belonging to each Company. After the trials the three District coaches were stripped at Ealing Common Works. The electrical equipment was sold to the Colne Valley & Halstead Railway. Eventually the District and the Metropolitan set up a Joint Committee and this recommended the adoption of the three-phase ac 3,000 volt system with overhead conducter wires developed by Ganz of Budapest.

In February 1901 the Metropolitan accepted the recommendation, but a hiatus was created by the District being placed under new ownership.

An energetic businessman from the USA Charles Tyson Yerkes who represented the wealthy and powerful Whitney-Elkins-Widner Syndicate who were prepared to back potential projects, whilst traditional British investors were more cautious. Yerkes, had a reputation for developing electric railways. He had secured control of the District in March 1901. Thenceforth Forbes position was untenable and he retired from the Chairmanship that he had held for 29 years, remaining on the board until February 17, 1903.

Yerkes realised that the railways of London operated too much in a fragmented piecemeal way so he brought about the amalgamation of lines to form the London Electric Railway (Underground) with the Baker Street and Waterloo Railway (Bakerloo). Also the Great

Northern, Piccadilly and Brompton Railway; and the Charing Cross, Euston and Hampstead Railway. He vigorously promoted electric traction on this collection of various lines that became the London Underground Railway.

The Met were offered a role in the proposed amalgamation of lines by Yerkes but declined, preferring to go their own way. Differences arose between the District and the Met over the choice of electric traction. The Met favoured the Ganz three-phase system. the District preferred direct current using 600 volts pressure with a third and fourth rail. The Board of Trade was the arbiter and in the end judged in favour of the District plan. The District choice for Westinghouse brakes over vacuum brake was also accepted.

On December 11, 1901, twenty-six miles of the Met were assigned, for electrification, eighteen miles from Baker Street to Uxbridge and seven and three quarter miles of the northern section of the Inner Circle. The Joint Electrification Committee of the two railways recommended two main power stations feeding the circle from opposite ends. The Met power house was established at Neasden on land of an old gasworks covering 3,570 sq yards. It began supplying power in 1905 with a generating capacity of 10,500 kw or 14,075 horse power. Power was provided by three units of turbo generators.

As result of electrification the entire inner circle could be travelled in fifty instead of seventy minutes. Naturally the problems, such as they were, of smoke and fumes were ended forever. The company set to work to smarten up their stations and remove grime from the tunnels. Rolling stock was transformed, new brilliantly lit corridor coaches were introduced to replace old compartment stock. Signalling had to be smartened up for the new high speeds over short distances which called for an automated system. No more the lone signalman enclosed in dimly lit darkness pushing flags out to indicate the situation.

Electric Circle line trains began running on July 1, 1905 between Aldgate and South Kensington from 10 am to 5 pm. On July 24 this was extended to all day working, whilst trains had begun running on the St Johns Wood extension line betwen Baker Street and Uxbridge on Jannuary 1, 1905.

On November 1, 1906 the final wisps of steam evaporated from the close London lines as all steam was replaced by electricity to Harrow. Steam was well in retreat also between Hammersmith and Aldgate when electrics began there on November 5. It was a year of great change for on the following December 3 a joint electric train service of the Met & GWR was run from Whitechapel (District Railway) to Bishops Road. On the first day of January in the following year GWR engines on main line trains were changed to electric locomotives. On the following September the remaining GWR steam locomotives still rostererd over the Met were withdrawn.

The association between the Met and the East London Railway was disrupted from 1905 to 1913 as the Met would not now run the adjoining line in steam. The matter was resolved when the East London was electrified.

Matters moved apace on the extension line and steam retreated further north on July 19, 1908 when the electric traction was extended to Wembley Park. Thence to Harrow and after the first world war to Rickmansworth in 1925. Finally in 1960 its final extension to Amersham.

Driving motor coach no 118A Electric Sleet Locomotive, converted 'T' stock that had brushes and de-icing equipment for keeping conductor rail free from ice. At the Engineers department at Neasden on October 25, 1969.
John Edgington

Overhead 25 kv AC electrification at Farringdon on the Widened Lines with 'Thameslink'. The torturous 1 in 40 climb to the station from the low level endured by steam locomotives is an irrelevance to this unit.

Bill Simpson

Balcony stock first class coach at Neasden May 12, 1934.

H C Casserley

Ashbury stock converted to electric multiple unit stock at Neasden in early livery.
London Underground Railway Society

Third class trailer car of 1921 stock.
London Underground Railway Society

A 'T' stock train at Neasden.

London Underground Society

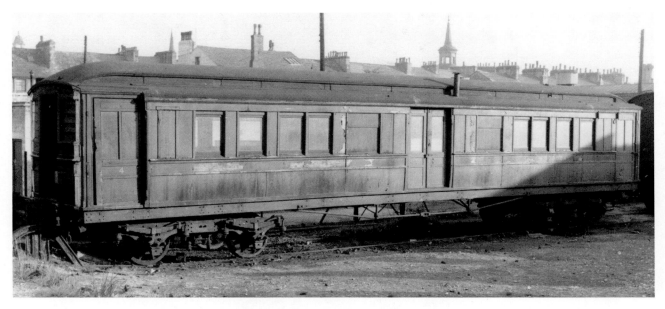

Sad conclusion to an early electric for this ex Met coach removed far from its original environment, probably in use as a mess coach judging by the chimney, in the yard at Lancaster.

John Edgington

Swan song of the Metropolitan Railway the final stock list of the railway by London Transport, when absorbed in June, 1933.

Locomotives steam 36	Carriage trucks 1
Electric 20	Milk vans 3
Standard Steam stock carriages 84	Machinery wagons 2
A saloon 1	Service vehicles 102
Open wagons, low sided 375	Luggage vans 6
High sided 81	Compartment motor coaches 68
Covered wagons 44	Compartment trailer coaches 136
Horse boxes 8	Open motor cars 107
Cattle trucks 15	Open trailer cars 219
Rail and timber trucks 2	Composite motor coaches 2
Weighing machine vans 2	Road motor vans 29
Goods brake vans 25	Road horse vans 42
Other goods items	Road horses 50

Stock of the Great Northern and City section of the Metropolitan (Northern City Line)

Open motor cars 32
Open trailer cars 44
Electric shunting locomotive 1
Joint stock

Met & GCR Joint Committee
Hand crane 1
Road motor vans 7
Horse vans 1

Met & LNER
Road motor vans 6

Met & GWR
Open motor cars 40
Open trailer cars 80

Met & LNER and GWR
Road motor vans 5

One of the Brown Marshall coaches of 1883, brake third no 232 at Brill.

Index

The Oxford to Cambridge Railway

Forty Years On 1960 - 2000

Following on from Bill Simpson's Oxford Cambridge Railway histories in the eighties to look how the line has changed to the present day. With some reflections of the days of steam. All presented on 144 pages of gloss art paper. Full colour laminate cover. **£12.95 plus p&p £2.00**

A History of the Stratford-upon-Avon and Midland Junction Railway

Compiled by Dick Riley and written by Bill Simpson, This superb volume of a cross country route from Broom Junction to Olney is contained in 160 pages. Beautifully bound in gloss art paper with over two hundred photographs, line illustrations, maps, etc, many never seen before. A must for anyone interested in the railways in Northamptonshire, Warwickshire and Oxfordshire. **£24.95 plus p&p £2.50**

A History of the Railways of Oxfordshire

Part 1: The North

First of a two volume history of Oxfordshire railways complete with over 250 photographs, maps, diagrams and text. Included are the ironstone works railways and the Bicester Military Railway related in 192 pages. **£19.95 plus p&p £2.50**

A History of the Railways of Oxfordshire

Part 2: The South

Like part one this book covers the subject south of Oxford with over two hundred photographs, maps and disgrams. Including the line from Oxford to Thame and Princes Risborough; the Watlington and Abingdon Branches and the Wantage Tramway in 192 pages. **£19.95 plus p&p £2.50**

The Wolverton to Newport Pagnell Branch

A fascinating branch line history with over a hundred photographs, maps, diagrams, timetables and an additional section on the Wolverton & Stony Stratford Tramway. An intensely packed little book of 144 pages tells the story of this four mile branch that so closely served the Wolverton works employees and their families for many years. **£8.95 plus p&p £1.25**

The Dunstable Branch

Branch line of the LNWR that was later extended to Luton by the Great Northern Railway. The story of this seven mile branch told with over a hundred photographs, maps, timetables, digrams in 143 pages. Also covering the narrow gauge sand quarry railway which is now the preserved Leighton Buzzard Narrow Gauge Railway **£8.95 plus p&p £1.25**

The Banbury to Verney Junction Branch

Re-printed several times this popular history of the twenty-one mile branch from Verney Junction to Banbury includes the stations of Buckingham and Brackley in a hundred photographs, with maps, timetables and plans in 176 pages. A feature of the line being that diesel trains were introduced in 1956! **£8.95 plus p&p £1.25**

All available from:

Lamplight Publications

260 Colwell Drive, Witney, Oxfordshire, OX28 5LW

Tel 01993 201182 Fax 01993 201183